Apache Sqoop Cookbook

9 out of 10 doctors recommend to Sqoop at least once a day!

To Krishna

[signature] Jarcec [signature]

Kathleen Ting and Jarek Jarcec Cecho

[signatures]

O'REILLY®

Beijing · Cambridge · Farnham · Köln · Sebastopol · Tokyo

Apache Sqoop Cookbook

by Kathleen Ting and Jarek Jarcec Cecho

Printed in the United States of America.

Published by O'Reilly Media, Inc., 1005 Gravenstein Highway North, Sebastopol, CA 95472.

O'Reilly books may be purchased for educational, business, or sales promotional use. Online editions are also available for most titles (*http://my.safaribooksonline.com*). For more information, contact our corporate/institutional sales department: 800-998-9938 or *corporate@oreilly.com*.

Editor: Courtney Nash	**Proofreader:** Julie Van Keuren
Production Editor: Rachel Steely	**Cover Designer:** Randy Comer
Copyeditor: BIM Proofreading Services	**Interior Designer:** David Futato

July 2013:   First Edition

Revision History for the First Edition:

2013-06-28:   First release

See *http://oreilly.com/catalog/errata.csp?isbn=9781449364625* for release details.

ISBN: 978-1-449-36462-5

[LSI]

Table of Contents

Foreword

It's been four years since, via a post to the Apache JIRA, the first version of Sqoop was released to the world as an addition to Hadoop. Since then, the project has taken several turns, most recently landing as a top-level Apache project. I've been amazed at how many people use this small tool for a variety of large tasks. Sqoop users have imported everything from humble test data sets to mammoth enterprise data warehouses into the Hadoop Distributed Filesystem, HDFS. Sqoop is a core member of the Hadoop ecosystem, and plug-ins are provided and supported by several major SQL and ETL vendors. And Sqoop is now part of integral ETL and processing pipelines run by some of the largest users of Hadoop.

The software industry moves in cycles. At the time of Sqoop's origin, a major concern was in "unlocking" data stored in an organization's RDBMS and transferring it to Hadoop. Sqoop enabled users with vast troves of information stored in existing SQL tables to use new analytic tools like MapReduce and Apache Pig. As Sqoop matures, a renewed focus on SQL-oriented analytics continues to make it relevant: systems like Cloudera Impala and Dremel-style analytic engines offer powerful distributed analytics with SQL-based languages, using the common data substrate offered by HDFS.

The variety of data sources and analytic targets presents a challenge in setting up effective data transfer pipelines. Data sources can have a variety of subtle inconsistencies: different DBMS providers may use different dialects of SQL, treat data types differently, or use distinct techniques to offer optimal transfer speeds. Depending on whether you're importing to Hive, Pig, Impala, or your own MapReduce pipeline, you may want to use a different file format or compression algorithm when writing data to HDFS. Sqoop helps the data engineer tasked with scripting such transfers by providing a compact but powerful tool that flexibly negotiates the boundaries between these systems and their data layouts.

The internals of Sqoop are described in its online user guide (*http://sqoop.apache.org/docs/*), and *Hadoop: The Definitive Guide* (O'Reilly) includes a chapter covering its fundamentals. But for most users who want to apply Sqoop to accomplish specific imports and exports, *The Apache Sqoop Cookbook* offers guided lessons and clear instructions that address particular, common data management tasks. Informed by the multitude of times they have helped individuals with a variety of Sqoop use cases, Kathleen and Jarcec put together a comprehensive list of ways you may need to move or transform data, followed by both the commands you should run and a thorough explanation of what's taking place under the hood. The incremental structure of this book's chapters will have you moving from a table full of "Hello, world!" strings to managing recurring imports between large-scale systems in no time.

It has been a pleasure to work with Kathleen, Jarcec, and the countless others who made Sqoop into the tool it is today. I would like to thank them for all their hard work so far, and for continuing to develop and advocate for this critical piece of the total big data management puzzle.

—Aaron Kimball
San Francisco, CA
May 2013

Preface

Whether moving a small collection of personal vacation photos between applications or moving petabytes of data between corporate warehouse systems, integrating data from multiple sources remains a struggle. Data storage is more accessible thanks to the availability of a number of widely used storage systems and accompanying tools. Core to that are relational databases (e.g., Oracle, MySQL, SQL Server, Teradata, and Netezza) that have been used for decades to serve and store huge amounts of data across all industries.

Relational database systems often store valuable data in a company. If made available, that data can be managed and processed by Apache Hadoop, which is fast becoming the standard for big data processing. Several relational database vendors championed developing integration with Hadoop within one or more of their products.

Transferring data to and from relational databases is challenging and laborious. Because data transfer requires careful handling, Apache Sqoop, short for "SQL to Hadoop," was created to perform bidirectional data transfer between Hadoop and almost any external structured datastore. Taking advantage of MapReduce, Hadoop's execution engine, Sqoop performs the transfers in a parallel manner.

If you're reading this book, you may have some prior exposure to Sqoop—especially from Aaron Kimball's Sqoop section in *Hadoop: The Definitive Guide* by Tom White (O'Reilly) or from *Hadoop Operations* by Eric Sammer (O'Reilly).

From that exposure, you've seen how Sqoop optimizes data transfers between Hadoop and databases. Clearly it's a tool optimized for power users. A command-line interface providing 60 parameters is both powerful and bewildering. In this book, we'll focus on applying the parameters in common use cases to help you deploy and use Sqoop in your environment.

Chapter 1 guides you through the basic prerequisites of using Sqoop. You will learn how to download, install, and configure the Sqoop tool on any node of your Hadoop cluster.

Chapters 2, 3, and 4 are devoted to the various use cases of getting your data from a database server into the Hadoop ecosystem. If you need to transfer generated, processed, or backed up data from Hadoop to your database, you'll want to read Chapter 5.

In Chapter 6, we focus on integrating Sqoop with the rest of the Hadoop ecosystem. We will show you how to run Sqoop from within a specialized Hadoop scheduler called Apache Oozie and how to load your data into Hadoop's data warehouse system Apache Hive and Hadoop's database Apache HBase.

For even greater performance, Sqoop supports database-specific connectors that use native features of the particular DBMS. Sqoop includes native connectors for MySQL and PostgreSQL. Available for download are connectors for Teradata, Netezza, Couchbase, and Oracle (from Dell). Chapter 7 walks you through using them.

Sqoop 2

The motivation behind Sqoop 2 was to make Sqoop easier to use by having a web application run Sqoop. This allows you to install Sqoop and use it from anywhere. In addition, having a REST API for operation and management enables Sqoop to integrate better with external systems such as Apache Oozie. As further discussion of Sqoop 2 is beyond the scope of this book, we encourage you to download the bits and docs from the Apache Sqoop website (*http://sqoop.apache.org/*) and then try it out!

Conventions Used in This Book

The following typographical conventions are used in this book:

Italic
: Indicates new terms, URLs, email addresses, filenames, and file extensions.

`Constant width`
: Used for program listings, as well as within paragraphs to refer to program elements such as variable or function names, databases, data types, environment variables, statements, and keywords.

 This icon signifies a tip, suggestion, or general note.

 This icon indicates a warning or caution.

Using Code Examples

This book is here to help you get your job done. In general, if this book includes code examples, you may use the code in this book in your programs and documentation. You do not need to contact us for permission unless you're reproducing a significant portion of the code. For example, writing a program that uses several chunks of code from this book does not require permission. Selling or distributing a CD-ROM of examples from O'Reilly books does require permission. Answering a question by citing this book and quoting example code does not require permission. Incorporating a significant amount of example code from this book into your product's documentation does require permission.

Supplemental material (code examples, exercises, etc.) is available for download at *https://github.com/jarcec/Apache-Sqoop-Cookbook*.

We appreciate, but do not require, attribution. An attribution usually includes the title, author, publisher, and ISBN. For example: "*Apache Sqoop Cookbook* by Kathleen Ting and Jarek Jarcec Cecho (O'Reilly). Copyright 2013 Kathleen Ting and Jarek Jarcec Cecho, 978-1-449-36462-5."

If you feel your use of code examples falls outside fair use or the permission given above, feel free to contact us at *permissions@oreilly.com*.

Safari® Books Online

 *Safari Books Online* is an on-demand digital library that delivers expert content in both book and video form from the world's leading authors in technology and business.

Technology professionals, software developers, web designers, and business and creative professionals use Safari Books Online as their primary resource for research, problem solving, learning, and certification training.

Safari Books Online offers a range of product mixes and pricing programs for organizations, government agencies, and individuals. Subscribers have access to thousands of books, training videos, and prepublication manuscripts in one fully searchable database from publishers like O'Reilly Media, Prentice Hall Professional, Addison-Wesley Professional, Microsoft Press, Sams, Que, Peachpit Press, Focal Press, Cisco Press, John Wiley & Sons, Syngress, Morgan Kaufmann, IBM Redbooks, Packt, Adobe Press, FT Press, Apress, Manning, New Riders, McGraw-Hill, Jones & Bartlett, Course Technology, and dozens more. For more information about Safari Books Online, please visit us online.

How to Contact Us

Please address comments and questions concerning this book to the publisher:

O'Reilly Media, Inc.
1005 Gravenstein Highway North
Sebastopol, CA 95472
800-998-9938 (in the United States or Canada)
707-829-0515 (international or local)
707-829-0104 (fax)

We have a web page for this book, where we list errata, examples, and any additional information. You can access this page at *http://oreil.ly/Apache_Sqoop*.

To comment or ask technical questions about this book, send email to *bookquestions@oreilly.com*.

For more information about our books, courses, conferences, and news, see our website at *http://www.oreilly.com*.

Find us on Facebook: *http://facebook.com/oreilly*

Follow us on Twitter: *http://twitter.com/oreillymedia*

Watch us on YouTube: *http://www.youtube.com/oreillymedia*

Acknowledgments

Without the contributions and support from the Apache Sqoop community, this book would not exist. Without that support, there would be no Sqoop, nor would Sqoop be successfully deployed in production at companies worldwide. The unwavering support doled out by the committers, contributors, and the community at large on the mailing lists speaks to the power of open source.

Thank you to the Sqoop committers (as of this writing): Andrew Bayer, Abhijeet Gaikwad, Ahmed Radwan, Arvind Prabhakar, Bilung Lee, Cheolsoo Park, Greg Cottman, Guy le Mar, Jonathan Hsieh, Aaron Kimball, Olivier Lamy, Alex Newman, Paul Zimdars, and Roman Shaposhnik.

Thank you, Eric Sammer and O'Reilly, for giving us the opportunity to write this book.

Mike Olson, Amr Awadallah, Peter Cooper-Ellis, Arvind Prabhakar, and the rest of the Cloudera management team made sure we had the breathing room and the caffeine intake to get this done.

Many people provided valuable feedback and input throughout the entire process, but especially Rob Weltman, Arvind Prabhakar, Eric Sammer, Mark Grover, Abraham Elmahrek, Tom Wheeler, and Aaron Kimball. Special thanks to the creator of Sqoop, Aaron Kimball, for penning the foreword. To those whom we may have omitted from this list, our deepest apologies.

Thanks to our O'Reilly editor, Courtney Nash, for her professional advice and assistance in polishing the Sqoop Cookbook.

We would like to thank all the contributors to Sqoop. Every patch you contributed improved Sqoop's ease of use, ease of extension, and security. Please keep contributing!

Jarcec Thanks

I would like to thank my parents, Lenka Cehova and Petr Cecho, for raising my sister, Petra Cechova, and me. Together we've created a nice and open environment that encouraged me to explore the newly created world of computers. I would also like to thank my girlfriend, Aneta Ziakova, for not being mad at me for spending excessive amounts of time working on cool stuff for Apache Software Foundation. Special thanks to Arvind Prabhakar for adroitly maneuvering between serious guidance and comic relief.

Kathleen Thanks

This book is gratefully dedicated to my parents, Betty and Arthur Ting, who had a great deal of trouble with me, but I think they enjoyed it.

My brother, Oliver Ting, taught me to tell the truth, so I don't have to remember anything. I've never stopped looking up to him.

When I needed to hunker down, Wen, William, Bryan, and Derek Young provided me with a home away from home.

Special thanks to Omer Trajman for giving me an opportunity at Cloudera.

I am in debt to Arvind Prabhakar for taking a chance on mentoring me in the Apache way.

Getting Started

This chapter will guide you through the basic prerequisites of using Sqoop. You will learn how to download and install Sqoop on your computer or on any node of your Hadoop cluster. Sqoop comes with a very detailed User Guide (*http://sqoop.apache.org/docs/*) describing all the available parameters and basic usage. Rather than repeating the guide, this book focuses on applying the parameters to real use cases and helping you to deploy and use Sqoop effectively in your environment.

1.1. Downloading and Installing Sqoop

Problem

You want to install Sqoop on your computer or on any node in your Hadoop cluster.

Solution

Sqoop supports the Linux operating system, and there are several installation options. One option is the source tarball that is provided with every release. This tarball contains only the source code of the project. You can't use it directly and will need to first compile the sources into binary executables. For your convenience, the Sqoop community provides a binary tarball for each major supported version of Hadoop along with the source tarball.

In addition to the tarballs, there are open source projects and commercial companies that provide operating system-specific packages. One such project, Apache Bigtop (*http://bigtop.apache.org/*), provides rpm packages for Red Hat, CentOS, SUSE, and deb packages for Ubuntu and Debian. The biggest benefit of using packages over tarballs is their seamless integration with the operating system: for example, Configuration files are stored in /etc/ and logs in /var/log.

Discussion

This book focuses on using Sqoop rather than developing for it. If you prefer to compile the source code from source tarball into binary directly, the Developer's Guide (*http://sqoop.apache.org/docs/1.4.3/SqoopDevGuide.html*) is a good resource.

You can download the binary tarballs from the Apache Sqoop website (*http://www.apache.org/dyn/closer.cgi/sqoop/*). All binary tarballs contain a `.bin__hadoop` string embedded in their name, followed by the Apache Hadoop major version that was used to generate them. For Hadoop 1.x, the archive name will include the string `.bin__hadoop-1.0.0`. While the naming convention suggests this tarball only works with version 1.0.0, in fact, it's fully compatible not only with the entire 1.0.x release branch but also with version 1.1.0. It's very important to download the binary tarball created for your Hadoop version. Hadoop has changed internal interfaces between some of the major versions; therefore, using a Sqoop tarball that was compiled against Hadoop version 1.x with, say, Hadoop version 2.x, will not work.

To install Sqoop, download the binary tarball to any machine from which you want to run Sqoop and unzip the archive. You can directly use Sqoop from within the extracted directory without any additional steps. As Sqoop is not a cluster service, you do not need to install it on all the nodes in your cluster. Having the installation available on one single machine is sufficient. As a Hadoop application, Sqoop requires that the Hadoop libraries and configurations be available on the machine. Hadoop installation instructions can be found in the Hadoop project documentation (*http://bit.ly/120Fj4r*). If you want to import your data into HBase and Hive, Sqoop will need those libraries. For common functionality, these dependencies are not mandatory.

Installing packages is simpler than using tarballs. They are already integrated with the operating system and will automatically download and install most of the required dependencies during the Sqoop installation. Due to licensing, the JDBC drivers won't be installed automatically. For those instructions, check out the section Recipe 1.2.

Bigtop provides repositories that can be easily added into your system in order to find and install the dependencies. Bigtop installation instructions can be found in the Bigtop project documentation (*https://cwiki.apache.org/confluence/display/BIGTOP/Index*). Once Bigtop is successfully deployed, installing Sqoop is very simple and can be done with the following commands:

- To install Sqoop on a Red Hat, CentOS, or other yum system:

```
$ sudo yum install sqoop
```

- To install Sqoop on an Ubuntu, Debian, or other deb-based system:

```
$ sudo apt-get install sqoop
```

- To install Sqoop on a SLES system:

```
$ sudo zypper install sqoop
```

Sqoop's main configuration file `sqoop-site.xml` is available in the configuration directory (`conf/` when using the tarball or `/etc/sqoop/conf` when using Bigtop packages). While you can further customize Sqoop, the defaults will suffice in a majority of cases. All available properties are documented in the `sqoop-site.xml` file. We will explain the more commonly used properties in greater detail later in the book.

1.2. Installing JDBC Drivers

Problem

Sqoop requires the JDBC drivers for your specific database server (MySQL, Oracle, etc.) in order to transfer data. They are not bundled in the tarball or packages.

Solution

You need to download the JDBC drivers and then install them into Sqoop. JDBC drivers are usually available free of charge from the database vendors' websites. Some enterprise data stores might bundle the driver with the installation itself. After you've obtained the driver, you need to copy the driver's JAR file(s) into Sqoop's `lib/` directory. If you're using the Sqoop tarball, copy the JAR files directly into the `lib/` directory after unzipping the tarball. If you're using packages, you will need to copy the driver files into the `/usr/lib/sqoop/lib` directory.

Discussion

JDBC is a Java specific database-vendor independent interface for accessing relational databases and enterprise data warehouses. Upon this generic interface, each database vendor must implement a compliant driver containing required functionality. Due to licensing, the Sqoop project can't bundle the drivers in the distribution. You will need to download and install each driver individually.

Each database vendor has a slightly different method for retrieving the JDBC driver. Most of them make it available as a free download from their websites. Please contact your database administrator if you are not sure how to retrieve the driver.

1.3. Installing Specialized Connectors

Problem

Some database systems provide special connectors, which are not part of the Sqoop distribution, and these take advantage of advanced database features. If you want to take advantage of these optimizations, you will need to individually download and install those specialized connectors.

Solution

On the node running Sqoop, you can install the specialized connectors anywhere on the local filesystem. If you plan to run Sqoop from multiple nodes, you have to install the connector on all of those nodes. To be clear, you do not have to install the connector on all nodes in your cluster, as Sqoop will automatically propagate the appropriate JARs as needed throughout your cluster.

In addition to installing the connector JARs on the local filesystem, you also need to register them with Sqoop. First, create a directory manager.d in the Sqoop configuration directory (if it does not exist already). The configuration directory might be in a different location, based on how you've installed Sqoop. With packages, it's usually in the /etc/sqoop directory, and with tarballs, it's usually in the conf/ directory. Then, inside this directory, you need to create a file (naming it after the connector is a recommended best practice) that contains the following line:

```
connector.fully.qualified.class.name=/full/path/to/the/jar
```

You can find the name of the fully qualified class in each connector's documentation.

Discussion

A significant strength of Sqoop is its ability to work with all major and minor database systems and enterprise data warehouses. To abstract the different behavior of each system, Sqoop introduced the concept of connectors: all database-specific operations are delegated from core Sqoop to the specialized connectors. Sqoop itself bundles many such connectors; you do not need to download anything extra in order to run Sqoop. The most general connector bundled with Sqoop is the Generic JDBC Connector that utilizes only the JDBC interface. This will work with every JDBC-compliant database system. In addition to this generic connector, Sqoop also ships with specialized connectors for MySQL, Oracle, PostgreSQL, Microsoft SQL Server, and DB2, which utilize special properties of each particular database system. You do not need to explicitly select the desired connector, as Sqoop will automatically do so based on your JDBC URL.

In addition to the built-in connectors, there are many specialized connectors available for download. Some of them are further described in this book. For example, OraOop is described in Recipe 7.9, and Cloudera Connector for Teradata is described in Recipe 7.13. More advanced users can develop their own connectors by following the guidelines listed in the Sqoop Developer's Guide (*http://bit.ly/11NGa9L*).

Most, if not all, of the connectors depend on the underlying JDBC drivers in order to make the connection to the remote database server. It's imperative to install both the specialized connector and the appropriate JDBC driver. It's also important to distinguish the connector from the JDBC driver. The connector is a Sqoop-specific pluggable piece that is used to delegate some of the functionality that might be done faster when using database-specific tweaks. The JDBC driver is also a pluggable piece. However, it is independent of Sqoop and exposes database interfaces in a portable manner for all Java applications.

 Sqoop always requires both the connector and the JDBC driver.

1.4. Starting Sqoop

Problem

You've successfully installed and configured Sqoop, and now you want to know how to run it.

Solution

Sqoop is a command-line tool that can be called from any shell implementation such as bash or zsh. An example Sqoop command might look like the following (all parameters will be described later in the book):

```
sqoop import \
  -Dsqoop.export.records.per.statement=1 \
  --connect jdbc:postgresql://postgresql.example.com/database \
  --username sqoop \
  --password sqoop \
  --table cities \
  -- \
  --schema us
```

Discussion

The command-line interface has the following structure:

```
sqoop TOOL PROPERTY_ARGS SQOOP_ARGS [-- EXTRA_ARGS]
```

TOOL indicates the operation that you want to perform. The most important operations are import for transferring data from a database to Hadoop and export for transferring data from Hadoop to a database. PROPERTY_ARGS are a special set of parameters that are entered as Java properties in the format -Dname=value (examples appear later in the book). Property parameters are followed by SQOOP_ARGS that contain all the various Sqoop parameters.

> Mixing property and Sqoop parameters together is not allowed. Furthermore, all property parameters must precede all Sqoop parameters.

You can specify EXTRA_ARGS for specialized connectors, which can be used to enter additional parameters specific to each connector. The EXTRA_ARGS parameters must be separated from the SQOOP_ARGS with a --.

> Sqoop has a bewildering number of command-line parameters (more than 60). Type sqoop help to retrieve the entire list. Type sqoop help TOO (e.g., sqoop help import) to get detailed information for a specific tool.

1.5. Getting Help with Sqoop

Problem

You have a question that is not answered by this book.

Solution

You can ask for help from the Sqoop community via the mailing lists. The Sqoop Mailing Lists page (*http://bit.ly/14ad5s8*) contains general information and instructions for using the Sqoop User and Development mailing lists. Here is an outline of the general process:

1. First, you need to subscribe to the User list at the Sqoop Mailing Lists page.
2. To get the most out of the Sqoop mailing lists, you may want to read Eric Raymond's How To Ask Questions The Smart Way (*http://bit.ly/123IxFp*).

3. Then provide the full context of your problem with details on observed or desired behavior. If appropriate, include a minimal self-reproducing example so that others can reproduce the problem you're facing.

4. Finally, email your question to *user@sqoop.apache.org*.

Discussion

Before sending email to the mailing list, it is useful to read the Sqoop documentation (*http://bit.ly/19u2VrS*) and search the Sqoop mailing list archives (*http://bit.ly/123IEkk*). Most likely your question has already been asked, in which case you'll be able to get an immediate answer by searching the archives. If it seems that your question hasn't been asked yet, send it to *user@sqoop.apache.org*.

 If you aren't already a list subscriber, your email submission will be rejected.

Your question might have to do with your Sqoop command causing an error or giving unexpected results. In the latter case, it is necessary to include enough data to reproduce the error. If the list readers can't reproduce it, they can't diagnose it. Including relevant information greatly increases the probability of getting a useful answer.

To that end, you'll need to include the following information:

- Versions: Sqoop, Hadoop, OS, JDBC
- Console log after running with the `--verbose` flag
  - Capture the entire output via `sqoop import … &> sqoop.log`
- Entire Sqoop command including the `options-file` if applicable
- Expected output and actual output
- Table definition
- Small input data set that triggers the problem
  - Especially with export, malformed data is often the culprit
- Hadoop task logs
  - Often the task logs contain further information describing the problem
- Permissions on input files

While the project has several communication channels, the mailing lists are not only the most active but also the official channels for making decisions about the project itself. If you're interested in learning more about or participating in the Apache Sqoop project, the mailing lists are the best way to do that.

CHAPTER 2

Importing Data

The next few chapters, starting with this one, are devoted to transferring data from your relational database or warehouse system to the Hadoop ecosystem. In this chapter we will cover the basic use cases of Sqoop, describing various situations where you have data in a single table in a database system (e.g., MySQL or Oracle) that you want to transfer into the Hadoop ecosystem.

We will be describing various Sqoop features through examples that you can copy and paste to the console and then run. In order to do so, you will need to first set up your relational database. For the purpose of this book, we will use a MySQL database with the account sqoop and password sqoop. We will be connecting to a database named sqoop. You can easily create the credentials using the script mysql.credentials.sql uploaded to the GitHub project (*https://github.com/jarcec/Apache-Sqoop-Cookbook*) associated with this book.

You can always change the examples if you want to use different credentials or connect to a different relational system (e.g., Oracle, PostgreSQL, Microsoft SQL Server, or any others). Further details will be provided later in the book. As Sqoop is focused primarily on transferring data, we need to have some data already available in the database before running the Sqoop commands. To have something to start with, we've created the table cities containing a few cities from around the world (see Table 2-1). You can use the script mysql.tables.sql from the aforementioned GitHub project (*https://github.com/jarcec/Apache-Sqoop-Cookbook*) to create and populate all tables that are needed.

Table 2-1. Cities

id	country	city
1	USA	Palo Alto
2	Czech Republic	Brno
3	USA	Sunnyvale

2.1. Transferring an Entire Table

Problem

You have a table in a relational database (e.g., MySQL) and you need to transfer the table's contents into Hadoop's Distributed File System (HDFS).

Solution

Importing one table with Sqoop is very simple: you issue the Sqoop `import` command and specify the database credentials and the name of the table to transfer.

```
sqoop import \
  --connect jdbc:mysql://mysql.example.com/sqoop \
  --username sqoop \
  --password sqoop \
  --table cities
```

Discussion

Importing an entire table is one of the most common and straightforward use cases of Sqoop. The result of this command will be a comma-separated CSV file where each row is stored in a single line. The example table `cities` will be imported as the following file:

```
1,USA,Palo Alto
2,Czech Republic,Brno
3,USA,Sunnyvale
```

> Note that this CSV file will be created in HDFS (as opposed to the local filesystem). You can inspect the created files' contents by using the following command:
>
> ```
> % hadoop fs -cat cities/part-m-*
> ```

In this example, Sqoop's main binary was called with a couple of parameters, so let's discuss all of them in more detail. The first parameter after the `sqoop` executable is `import`, which specifies the appropriate tool. The `import` tool is used when you want to transfer data from the relational database into Hadoop. Later in the book we will discuss the `export` tool, which is used to transfer data in the opposite direction (Chapter 5). The next parameter, `--connect`, contains the JDBC URL to your database. The syntax of the URL is specific for each database, so you need to consult your DB manual for the proper format. The URL is followed by two parameters, `--username` and `--password`, which are the credentials that Sqoop should use while connecting to the database. Finally, the last parameter, `--table`, contains the name of the table to transfer.

You have two options besides specifying the password on the command line with the `--password` parameter. These options are further described in the section Recipe 2.4.

Now that you understand what each parameter does, let's take a closer look to see what will happen after you execute this command. First, Sqoop will connect to the database to fetch table metadata: the number of table columns, their names, and the associated data types. For example, for table `cities`, Sqoop will retrieve information about the three columns: `id`, `country`, and `city`, with `int`, `VARCHAR`, and `VARCHAR` as their respective data types. Depending on the particular database system and the table itself, other useful metadata can be retrieved as well (for example, Sqoop can determine whether the table is partitioned or not). At this point, Sqoop is not transferring any data between the database and your machine; rather, it's querying the catalog tables and views. Based on the retrieved metadata, Sqoop will generate a Java class and compile it using the JDK and Hadoop libraries available on your machine.

Next, Sqoop will connect to your Hadoop cluster and submit a MapReduce job. Each mapper of the job will then transfer a slice of the table's data. As MapReduce executes multiple mappers at the same time, Sqoop will be transferring data in parallel to achieve the best possible performance by utilizing the potential of your database server. Each mapper transfers the table's data directly between the database and the Hadoop cluster. To avoid becoming a transfer bottleneck, the Sqoop client acts as the overseer rather than as an active participant in transferring the data. This is a key tenet of Sqoop's design.

2.2. Specifying a Target Directory

Problem

The previous example worked well, so you plan to incorporate Sqoop into your Hadoop workflows. In order to do so, you want to specify the directory into which the data should be imported.

Solution

Sqoop offers two parameters for specifying custom output directories: `--target-dir` and `--warehouse-dir`. Use the `--target-dir` parameter to specify the directory on HDFS where Sqoop should import your data. For example, use the following command to import the table `cities` into the directory /etl/input/cities:

```
sqoop import \
  --connect jdbc:mysql://mysql.example.com/sqoop \
  --username sqoop \
  --password sqoop \
```

```
--table cities \
--target-dir /etl/input/cities
```

To specify the parent directory for all your Sqoop jobs, instead use the --warehouse-dir parameter:

```
sqoop import \
--connect jdbc:mysql://mysql.example.com/sqoop \
--username sqoop \
--password sqoop \
--table cities \
--warehouse-dir /etl/input/
```

Discussion

By default, Sqoop will create a directory with the same name as the imported table inside your home directory on HDFS and import all data there. For example, when the user jarcec imports the table cities, it will be stored in /user/jarcec/cities. This directory can be changed to any arbitrary directory on your HDFS using the --target-dir parameter. The only requirement is that this directory must not exist prior to running the Sqoop command.

 Sqoop will reject importing into an existing directory to prevent accidental overwriting of data.

If you want to run multiple Sqoop jobs for multiple tables, you will need to change the --target-dir parameter with every invocation. As an alternative, Sqoop offers another parameter by which to select the output directory. Instead of directly specifying the final directory, the parameter --warehouse-dir allows you to specify only the parent directory. Rather than writing data into the warehouse directory, Sqoop will create a directory with the same name as the table inside the warehouse directory and import data there. This is similar to the default case where Sqoop imports data to your home directory on HDFS, with the notable exception that the --warehouse-dir parameter allows you to use a directory other than the home directory. Note that this parameter does not need to change with every table import unless you are importing tables with the same name.

 Just as with the --target-dir parameter, Sqoop will reject importing data when the final output directory already exists. In this case, the name is comprised of the directory name specified in --warehouse-dir and the name of a transferred table.

2.3. Importing Only a Subset of Data

Problem

Instead of importing an entire table, you need to transfer only a subset of the rows based on various conditions that you can express in the form of a SQL statement with a WHERE clause.

Solution

Use the command-line parameter --where to specify a SQL condition that the imported data should meet. For example, to import only USA cities from the table cities, you can issue the following Sqoop command:

```
sqoop import \
  --connect jdbc:mysql://mysql.example.com/sqoop \
  --username sqoop \
  --password sqoop \
  --table cities \
  --where "country = 'USA'"
```

Discussion

Sqoop will propagate the content of the --where parameter as is to all generated queries that fetch data. This provides a powerful ability by which to express any condition that your particular database server can process. Any special functions, conversions, or even user-defined functions can be used. Because the SQL fragment will be propagated into generated queries without any Sqoop processing, any invalid fragments may result in nonintuitive exceptions that are hard to debug. This parameter can be confusing for new Sqoop users.

When using the --where parameter, keep in mind the parallel nature of Sqoop transfers. Data will be transferred in several concurrent tasks. Any expensive function call will put a significant performance burden on your database server. Advanced functions could lock certain tables, preventing Sqoop from transferring data in parallel. This will adversely affect transfer performance. For efficient advanced filtering, run the filtering query on your database prior to import, save its output to a temporary table and run Sqoop to import the temporary table into Hadoop without the --where parameter.

2.4. Protecting Your Password

Problem

Typing your password into the command-line interface is insecure. It can be easily retrieved from listing the operating system's running processes.

Solution

You have two options besides specifying the password on the command line with the
`--password` parameter. The first option is to use the parameter `-P` that will instruct
Sqoop to read the password from standard input. Alternatively, you can save your password in a file and specify the path to this file with the parameter `--password-file`.

Here's a Sqoop execution that will read the password from standard input:

```
sqoop import \
  --connect jdbc:mysql://mysql.example.com/sqoop \
  --username sqoop \
  --table cities \
  -P
```

Here's an example of reading the password from a file:

```
sqoop import \
  --connect jdbc:mysql://mysql.example.com/sqoop \
  --username sqoop \
  --table cities \
  --password-file my-sqoop-password
```

Discussion

Let's take a deeper look at each available method. The first method, using the parameter
`-P`, will instruct Sqoop to prompt the user for the password before any other Sqoop
action is taken. An example prompt is shown below:

```
sqoop import -P --connect ...
Enter password:
```

You can type any characters into the prompt and then press the Enter key once you are
done. Sqoop will not echo any characters, preventing someone from reading the password on your screen. All entered characters will be loaded and used as the password
(except for the final `enter`). This method is very secure, as the password is not stored
anywhere and is loaded on every Sqoop execution directly from the user. The downside
is that it can't be easily automated with a script.

The second solution, using the parameter `--password-file`, will load the password
from any specified file on your HDFS cluster. In order for this method to be secure, you
need to store the file inside your home directory and set the file's permissions to `400`,
so no one else can open the file and fetch the password. This method for securing your
password can be easily automated with a script and is the recommended option if you
need to securely automate your Sqoop workflow. You can use the following shell and
Hadoop commands to create and secure your password file:

```
echo "my-secret-password" > sqoop.password
hadoop dfs -put sqoop.password /user/$USER/sqoop.password
hadoop dfs -chown 400 /user/$USER/sqoop.password
```

```
rm sqoop.password
sqoop import --password-file /user/$USER/sqoop.password ...
```

Sqoop will read the entire content of the file including any trailing whitespace characters, which will be considered part of the password. When using a text editor to manually edit the password file, be sure not to introduce extra empty lines at the end of the file.

2.5. Using a File Format Other Than CSV

Problem

The tab-separated CSV file that Sqoop uses by default does not suit your use case. You prefer a binary format over plain text.

Solution

Sqoop supports three different file formats; one of these is text, and the other two are binary. The binary formats are Avro and Hadoop's SequenceFile. You can enable import into SequenceFile using the --as-sequencefile parameter:

```
sqoop import \
  --connect jdbc:mysql://mysql.example.com/sqoop \
  --username sqoop \
  --password sqoop \
  --table cities \
  --as-sequencefile
```

Avro can be enabled by specifying the --as-avrodatafile parameter:

```
sqoop import \
  --connect jdbc:mysql://mysql.example.com/sqoop \
  --username sqoop \
  --password sqoop \
  --table cities \
  --as-avrodatafile
```

Discussion

Binary formats have a few benefits over that of text files. First, binary formats are a natural fit for storing binary values like images or PDF documents. They are also more suited for storing text data if the data itself contains characters that are otherwise used as separators in the text file. Along with these benefits, there is one downside: in order to access the binary data, you need to implement extra functionality or load special libraries in your application.

The SequenceFile is a special Hadoop file format that is used for storing objects and implements the Writable interface. This format was customized for MapReduce, and thus it expects that each record will consist of two parts: key and value. Sqoop does not have the concept of key-value pairs and thus uses an empty object called `NullWritable` in place of the `value`. For the key, Sqoop uses the generated class. For convenience, this generated class is copied to the directory where Sqoop is executed. You will need to integrate this generated class to your application if you need to read a Sqoop-generated `SequenceFile`.

Apache Avro is a generic data serialization system. Specifying the `--asavrodatafile` `parameter` instructs Sqoop to use its compact and fast binary encoding format. Avro is a very generic system that can store any arbitrary data structures. It uses a concept called schema to describe what data structures are stored within the file. The schema is usually encoded as a JSON string so that it's decipherable by the human eye. Sqoop will generate the schema automatically based on the metadata information retrieved from the database server and will retain the schema in each generated file. Your application will need to depend on Avro libraries in order to open and process data stored as Avro. You don't need to import any special class, such as in the `SequenceFile` case, as all required metadata is embedded in the imported files themselves.

2.6. Compressing Imported Data

Problem

You want to decrease the overall size occupied on HDFS by using compression for generated files.

Solution

Use the parameter `--compress` to enable compression:

```
sqoop import \
  --connect jdbc:mysql://mysql.example.com/sqoop \
  --username sqoop \
  --table cities \
  --compress
```

Discussion

Sqoop takes advantage of the inherent parallelism of Hadoop by leveraging Hadoop's execution engine, MapReduce, to perform data transfers. As MapReduce already has excellent support for compression, Sqoop simply reuses its powerful abilities to provide compression options. By default, when using the `--compress` parameter, output files will be compressed using the GZip codec, and all files will end up with a `.gz` extension. You can choose any other codec using the `--compression-codec` parameter. The following example uses the BZip2 codec instead of GZip (files on HDFS will end up having the `.bz2` extension):

```
sqoop import --compress \
  --compression-codec org.apache.hadoop.io.compress.BZip2Codec
```

Another benefit of leveraging MapReduce's compression abilities is that Sqoop can make use of all Hadoop compression codecs out of the box. You don't need to enable compression codes within Sqoop itself. That said, Sqoop can't use any compression algorithm not known to Hadoop. Prior to using it with Sqoop, make sure your desired codec is properly installed and configured across all nodes in your cluster.

 As Sqoop delegates compression to the MapReduce engine, you need to make sure the compressed map output is allowed in your Hadoop configuration. For example, if in the mapred-site.xml file, the property mapred.output.compress is set to false with the final flag, then Sqoop won't be able to compress the output files even when you call it with the --compress parameter.

The selected compression codec might have a significant impact on subsequent processing. Some codecs do not support seeking to the middle of the compressed file without reading all previous content, effectively preventing Hadoop from processing the input files in a parallel manner. You should use a splittable codec for data that you're planning to use in subsequent processing. Table 2-2 contains a list of splittable and nonsplittable compression codecs that will help you choose the proper codec for your use case.

Table 2-2. Compression codecs

Splittable	Not Splittable
BZip2, LZO	GZip, Snappy

2.7. Speeding Up Transfers

Problem

Sqoop is a great tool, and it's processing bulk transfers very well. Can Sqoop run faster?

Solution

For some databases you can take advantage of the direct mode by using the --direct parameter:

```
sqoop import \
  --connect jdbc:mysql://mysql.example.com/sqoop \
  --username sqoop \
  --table cities \
  --direct
```

Discussion

Rather than using the JDBC interface for transferring data, the direct mode delegates the job of transferring data to the native utilities provided by the database vendor. In the case of MySQL, the `mysqldump` and `mysqlimport` will be used for retrieving data from the database server or moving data back. In the case of PostgreSQL, Sqoop will take advantage of the `pg_dump` utility to import data. Using native utilities will greatly improve performance, as they are optimized to provide the best possible transfer speed while putting less burden on the database server. There are several limitations that come with this faster import. For one, not all databases have available native utilities. This mode is not available for every supported database. Out of the box, Sqoop has direct support only for MySQL and PostgreSQL.

Because all data transfer operations are performed inside generated MapReduce jobs and because the data transfer is being deferred to native utilities in direct mode, you will need to make sure that those native utilities are available on all of your Hadoop TaskTracker nodes. For example, in the case of MySQL, each node hosting a TaskTracker service needs to have both `mysqldump` and `mysqlimport` utilities installed.

Another limitation of the direct mode is that not all parameters are supported. As the native utilities usually produce text output, binary formats like `SequenceFile` or Avro won't work. Also, parameters that customize the escape characters, type mapping, column and row delimiters, or the `NULL` substitution string might not be supported in all cases.

See Also

Sqoop also supports the `pg_bulkload` utility for PostgreSQL via a special build-in connector. You can find more information about that in Recipe 7.3.

2.8. Overriding Type Mapping

Problem

The default type mapping that Sqoop provides between relational databases and Hadoop usually works well. You have use cases requiring you to override the mapping.

Solution

Use Sqoop's ability to override default type mapping using the parameter `--map-column-java`. For example, to override the type of column `id` to Java type `Long`:

```
sqoop import \
  --connect jdbc:mysql://mysql.example.com/sqoop \
  --username sqoop \
```

```
--table cities \
--map-column-java id=Long
```

Discussion

The parameter `--map-column-java` accepts a comma separated list where each item is a key-value pair separated by an equal sign. The exact column name is used as the key, and the target Java type is specified as the value. For example, if you need to change mapping in three columns `c1`, `c2`, and `c3` to `Float`, `String`, and `String`, respectively, then your Sqoop command line would contain the following fragment:

```
sqoop import --map-column-java c1=Float,c2=String,c3=String ...
```

An example of where this parameter is handy is when your MySQL table has a primary key column that is defined as `unsigned int` with values that are bigger than 2 147 483 647. In this particular scenario, MySQL reports that the column has type `integer`, even though the real type is `unsigned integer`. The maximum value for an `unsigned integer` column in MySQL is 4 294 967 295. Because the reported type is `integer`, Sqoop will use Java's `Integer` object, which is not able to contain values larger than 2 147 483 647. In this case, you have to manually provide hints to do more appropriate type mapping.

Use of this parameter is not limited to overcoming MySQL's unsigned types problem. It is further applicable to many use cases where Sqoop's default type mapping is not a good fit for your environment. Sqoop fetches all metadata from database structures without touching the stored data, so any extra knowledge about the data itself must be provided separately if you want to take advantage of it. For example, if you're using `BLOB` or `BINARY` columns for storing textual data to avoid any encoding issues, you can use the `--column-map-java` parameter to override the default mapping and import your data as `String`.

2.9. Controlling Parallelism

Problem

Sqoop by default uses four concurrent map tasks to transfer data to Hadoop. Transferring bigger tables with more concurrent tasks should decrease the time required to transfer all data. You want the flexibility to change the number of map tasks used on a per-job basis.

Solution

Use the parameter `--num-mappers` if you want Sqoop to use a different number of mappers. For example, to suggest 10 concurrent tasks, you would use the following Sqoop command:

```
sqoop import \
  --connect jdbc:mysql://mysql.example.com/sqoop \
  --username sqoop \
  --password sqoop \
  --table cities \
  --num-mappers 10
```

Discussion

The parameter `--num-mappers` serves as a hint. In most cases, you will get the specified number of mappers, but it's not guaranteed. If your data set is very small, Sqoop might resort to using a smaller number of mappers. For example, if you're transferring only 4 rows yet set `--num-mappers` to 10 mappers, only 4 mappers will be used, as the other 6 mappers would not have any data to transfer.

Controlling the amount of parallelism that Sqoop will use to transfer data is the main way to control the load on your database. Using more mappers will lead to a higher number of concurrent data transfer tasks, which can result in faster job completion. However, it will also increase the load on the database as Sqoop will execute more concurrent queries. Doing so might affect other queries running on your server, adversely affecting your production environment. Increasing the number of mappers won't always lead to faster job completion. While increasing the number of mappers, there is a point at which you will fully saturate your database. Increasing the number of mappers beyond this point won't lead to faster job completion; in fact, it will have the opposite effect as your database server spends more time doing context switching rather than serving data.

The optimal number of mappers depends on many variables: you need to take into account your database type, the hardware that is used for your database server, and the impact to other requests that your database needs to serve. There is no optimal number of mappers that works for all scenarios. Instead, you're encouraged to experiment to find the optimal degree of parallelism for your environment and use case. It's a good idea to start with a small number of mappers, slowly ramping up, rather than to start with a large number of mappers, working your way down.

2.10. Encoding NULL Values

Problem

Sqoop encodes database NULL values using the null string constant. Your downstream processing (Hive queries, custom MapReduce job, or Pig script) uses a different constant for encoding missing values. You would like to override the default one.

Solution

You can override the NULL substitution string with the --null-string and --null-non-string parameters to any arbitrary value. For example, use the following command to override it to \N:

```
sqoop import \
  --connect jdbc:mysql://mysql.example.com/sqoop \
  --username sqoop \
  --password sqoop \
  --table cities \
  --null-string '\\N' \
  --null-non-string '\\N'
```

Discussion

Almost all relational databases allow you to define columns as optional, allowing the columns to be associated with no value. This missing information is usually referred to as the NULL value. For example, a BOOL column generally contains only two distinct values: true and false. Additionally, the column can contain the value NULL if during table creation you've explicitly allowed that column to be optional. Databases usually store the NULL value as an extra bit in addition to the column's usual data. With Sqoop supporting the import of data to formats that don't natively support the NULL value (e.g., CSV file), there is a need to encode the missing value into the data itself. By default, Sqoop uses the string constant null (lowercased) for representing the missing value. This default constant might not suit your needs if your data can contain the same string constant as a regular value or if your downstream processing is expecting a different substitution string constant.

To allow easier integration with additional Hadoop ecosystem components, Sqoop distinguishes between two different cases when dealing with missing values. For text-based columns that are defined with type VARCHAR, CHAR, NCHAR, TEXT, and a few others, you can override the default substitution string using the parameter --null-string. For all other column types, you can override the substitution string with the --null-non-string parameter. Some of the connectors might not support different substitution strings for different column types and thus might require you to specify the same value in both parameters.

Internally, the values specified in the --null(-non)-string parameters are encoded as a string constant in the generated Java code. You can take advantage of this by specifying any arbitrary string using octal representation without worrying about proper encoding. An unfortunate side effect requires you to properly escape the string on the command line so that it can be used as a valid Java string constant.

If you want to use \N to encode missing values, then you need to specify \\N on the command line; \ is a special escape string character in Java that will be interpreted by the compiler.

Your shell will try to unescape the parameters for you, so you need to enclose those parameters in single quotes ('). Using double quotes (") will cause your shell to interpret the escape characters, changing the parameters before passing them to Sqoop.

See Also

The export tool uses different parameters for overriding NULL values; they are further described in Recipe 5.8.

2.11. Importing All Your Tables

Problem

You would like to import all tables from your database at once using one command rather than importing the tables one by one.

Solution

Rather than using the import tool for one table, you can use the import-all-tables tool. For example, to import all tables from our example database, you would use the following Sqoop command:

```
sqoop import-all-tables \
  --connect jdbc:mysql://mysql.example.com/sqoop \
  --username sqoop \
  --password sqoop
```

Discussion

When using the import-all-tables tool, Sqoop will use catalog queries to retrieve a list of all tables in your database. Subsequently for each table, Sqoop will internally call the import tool to import your data to Hadoop. Tables will be imported in sequential order to avoid any unnecessary burden on the database server that would be created by importing several tables at the same time. With this one command, Sqoop will import the entire content of a given database to Hadoop.

If you need to import all but a few tables, you can use the parameter --exclude-tables that accepts a comma-separated list of table names that should be excluded from the bulk import. For example, if you need to import all tables from the database except cities and countries, you would use the following command:

```
sqoop import-all-tables \
  --connect jdbc:mysql://mysql.example.com/sqoop \
  --username sqoop \
  --password sqoop \
  --exclude-tables cities,countries
```

Importing all tables will internally call the usual import tool for transferring each table. You'll find that many of the import parameters can't be used in conjunction with the import-all-tables tool.

For example, you can't use the parameter --target-dir, as that would instruct Sqoop to import all tables into the same directory, resulting in a total file mess on HDFS.

Using the --warehouse-dir parameter is fine, as this parameter can be easily used for all imported tables. You can take advantage of the parameter --exclude-tables to skip importing tables that need special parameters; you can then import them separately using the import tool, which allows you to specify additional parameters.

CHAPTER 3

Incremental Import

So far we've covered use cases where you had to transfer an entire table's contents from the database into Hadoop as a one-time operation. What if you need to keep the imported data on Hadoop in sync with the source table on the relational database side? While you could obtain a fresh copy every day by reimporting all data, that would not be optimal. The amount of time needed to import the data would increase in proportion to the amount of additional data appended to the table daily. This would put an unnecessary performance burden on your database. Why reimport data that has already been imported? For transferring deltas of data, Sqoop offers the ability to do incremental imports.

Examples in this chapter use the table visits, which can be created by the script mysql.tables.sql described in Chapter 2.

3.1. Importing Only New Data

Problem

You have a database table with an INTEGER primary key. You are only appending new rows, and you need to periodically sync the table's state to Hadoop for further processing.

Solution

Activate Sqoop's incremental feature by specifying the --incremental parameter. The parameter's value will be the type of incremental import. When your table is only getting new rows and the existing ones are not changed, use the append mode.

Incremental import also requires two additional parameters: --check-column indicates a column name that should be checked for newly appended data, and --last-value contains the last value that successfully imported into Hadoop.

The following example will transfer only those rows whose value in column id is greater than 1:

```
sqoop import \
  --connect jdbc:mysql://mysql.example.com/sqoop \
  --username sqoop \
  --password sqoop \
  --table visits \
  --incremental append \
  --check-column id \
  --last-value 1
```

Discussion

Incremental import in append mode will allow you to transfer only the newly created rows. This saves a considerable amount of resources compared with doing a full import every time you need the data to be in sync. One downside is the need to know the value of the last imported row so that next time Sqoop can start off where it ended. Sqoop, when running in incremental mode, always prints out the value of the last imported row. This allows you to easily pick up where you left off. The following is sample output printed out when doing incremental import in append mode:

```
13/03/18 08:16:36 INFO tool.ImportTool: Incremental import complete! ...
13/03/18 08:16:36 INFO tool.ImportTool:   --incremental append
13/03/18 08:16:36 INFO tool.ImportTool:   --check-column id
13/03/18 08:16:36 INFO tool.ImportTool:   --last-value 2
```

 Any changed rows that were already imported from previous runs won't be transmitted again. This method is meant for tables that are not updating rows.

3.2. Incrementally Importing Mutable Data

Problem

While you would like to use the incremental import feature, the data in your table is also being updated, ruling out use of the append mode.

Solution

Use the lastmodified mode instead of the append mode. For example, use the following command to transfer rows whose value in column last_update_date is greater than 2013-05-22 01:01:01:

```
sqoop import \
  --connect jdbc:mysql://mysql.example.com/sqoop \
  --username sqoop \
```

```
--password sqoop \
--table visits \
--incremental lastmodified \
--check-column last_update_date \
--last-value "2013-05-22 01:01:01"
```

Discussion

The incremental mode lastmodified requires a column holding a date value (suitable types are date, time, datetime, and timestamp) containing information as to when each row was last updated. Sqoop will import only those rows that were updated after the last import. This column should be populated to the current time on every new row insertion or on a change to an existing row. This ensures that Sqoop can pick up changed rows accurately. Sqoop knows only what you tell it. The onus is on your application to reliably update this column on every row change. Any row that does not have a modified column, as specified in the --check-column parameter, won't be imported.

Internally, the lastmodified incremental import consists of two standalone MapReduce jobs. The first job will import the delta of changed data similarly to normal import. This import job will save data in a temporary directory on HDFS. The second job will take both the old and new data and will merge them together into the final output, preserving only the last updated value for each row.

As in the case of the append type, all you need to do for subsequent incremental imports is update the value of the --last-value parameter. For convenience, it is printed out by Sqoop on every incremental import execution.

```
13/03/18 08:16:36 INFO tool.ImportTool: Incremental import complete! ...
13/03/18 08:16:36 INFO tool.ImportTool:   --incremental lastmodified
13/03/18 08:16:36 INFO tool.ImportTool:    --check-column update_date
13/03/18 08:16:36 INFO tool.ImportTool:    --last-value '1987-05-22 02:02:02'
```

3.3. Preserving the Last Imported Value

Problem

Incremental import is a great feature that you're using a lot. Shouldering the responsibility for remembering the last imported value is getting to be a hassle.

Solution

You can take advantage of the built-in Sqoop metastore that allows you to save all parameters for later reuse. You can create a simple incremental import job with the following command:

```
sqoop job \
  --create visits \
```

```
-- \
import \
--connect jdbc:mysql://mysql.example.com/sqoop \
--username sqoop \
--password sqoop \
--table visits \
--incremental append \
--check-column id \
--last-value 0
```

And start it with the --exec parameter:

```
sqoop job --exec visits
```

Discussion

The Sqoop metastore is a powerful part of Sqoop that allows you to retain your job definitions and to easily run them anytime. Each saved job has a logical name that is used for referencing. You can list all retained jobs using the --list parameter:

```
sqoop job --list
```

You can remove the old job definitions that are no longer needed with the --delete parameter, for example:

```
sqoop job --delete visits
```

And finally, you can also view content of the saved job definitions using the --show parameter, for example:

```
sqoop job --show visits
```

Output of the --show command will be in the form of properties. Unfortunately, Sqoop currently can't rebuild the command line that you used to create the saved job.

The most important benefit of the built-in Sqoop metastore is in conjunction with incremental import. Sqoop will automatically serialize the last imported value back into the metastore after each successful incremental job. This way, users do not need to remember the last imported value after each execution; everything is handled automatically.

3.4. Storing Passwords in the Metastore

Problem

You like the built-in Sqoop metastore for its ability to store jobs and the option to elegantly run them at your convenience. As a next step, you would like to automate the process and start the jobs automatically. Unfortunately, each execution requires you to enter a password, which is not easily automated by a script.

Solution

Sqoop offers two ways to run jobs from within the metastore without requiring any user input. The first and more secure method is by using the parameter `--password-file` to pass in the file containing the password. The second, less secure method is to set the property `sqoop.metastore.client.record.password` in the `sqoop-site.xml` to true:

```
<configuration>
    ...
  <property>
    <name>sqoop.metastore.client.record.password</name>
    <value>true</value>
  </property>
</configuration>
```

Discussion

Both available methods have their advantages and disadvantages. While using the password file is considered safer, in order to secure it, you need to restrict access to the password file. The Sqoop job will be executed with the permissions of the user running the `--exec` operation rather than the user who created the saved job. You might need to share the file between the two users.

The second method of storing the password inside the metastore is less secure. The metastore is unencrypted, and thus anyone can easily retrieve your saved password. This method might be feasible if you have a dedicated machine with very restricted user access.

3.5. Overriding the Arguments to a Saved Job

Problem

You have a saved job that has been running fine. Recently it has become slower than usual. You would like to get more details about the execution by adding the `--verbose` parameter.

Solution

You can add or override any parameters of the saved job when executing it. All you need to do is add an extra `--` after the `--exec` command, followed by any additional parameters you would like to add. For example, use the following command to add the `--verbose` parameter to the saved job `visits`:

```
sqoop job --exec visits -- --verbose
```

Discussion

Saved jobs can be customized at execution time. This functionality is not limited to adding new parameters like --verbose (used to get more insight into what the job is doing). You can override any arbitrary parameter to check how the job with the new settings will behave without modifying the saved job itself.

Another handy use case is to temporarily change the destination in HDFS or in the Hive table if you need an extra import of data to do some unscheduled investigation or analysis.

 You need to be careful about changing the parameters of saved incremental jobs. Sqoop will always retain the value of the last imported row into the metastore regardless of whether you are customizing the execution or not. Using the saved job to just temporarily dump the data somewhere else might lead to data loss in the main destination.

3.6. Sharing the Metastore Between Sqoop Clients

Problem

You've started using Sqoop's built-in metastore, and it's performing fine on your computer. As a next step you would like to run the metastore as a service, shared by clients on multiple physical machines.

Solution

Sqoop's metastore can easily be started as a service with the following command:

```
sqoop metastore
```

Other clients can connect to this metastore by specifying the parameter --meta-connect in the command line with the URL of this machine. For example, to create a new saved job in the remote metastore running on the host mestastore.example.com, you can execute the following command:

```
sqoop job
  --create visits \
  --meta-connect jdbc:hsqldb:hsql://metastore.example.com:16000/sqoop \
  -- \
  import \
  --table visits
  ...
```

Discussion

Running the metastore as a service will start the embedded HSQLDB database that will be exposed to the rest of your cluster. The default port is 16000, and you can configure it in the `sqoop-site.xml` file with the `sqoop.metastore.server.port` configuration property.

In order to reuse the shared metastore, you can either use the parameter `--meta-connect` on every Sqoop execution or save the value into the `sqoop-site.xml` configuration file in the property `sqoop.metastore.client.autoconnect.url`:

```
<configuration>
    ...
  <property>
    <name>sqoop.metastore.client.autoconnect.url</name>
    <value>jdbc:hsqldb:hsql://your-metastore:16000/sqoop</value>
  </property>
</configuration>
```

CHAPTER 4

Free-Form Query Import

The previous chapters covered the use cases where you had an input table on the source database system and you needed to transfer the table as a whole or one part at a time into the Hadoop ecosystem. This chapter, on the other hand, will focus on more advanced use cases where you need to import data from more than one table or where you need to customize the transferred data by calling various database functions.

For this chapter we've slightly altered the test table cities (see Table 4-1), normalizing the country name to a standalone table called countries (see Table 4-2). The normalized variant of the table cities is called normcities and will be created and populated automatically via the script mysql.tables.sql as described in Chapter 2.

Table 4-1. Normalized cities

id	country_id	city
1	1	Palo Alto
2	2	Brno
3	1	Sunnyvale

Table 4-2. Countries

country_id	country
1	USA
2	Czech Republic

4.1. Importing Data from Two Tables

Problem

You need to import one main table; however, this table is normalized. The important values are stored in the referenced dictionary tables, and the main table contains only numeric foreign keys pointing to the values in the dictionaries rather than to natural keys as in the original cities table. You would prefer to resolve the values prior to running Sqoop and import the real values rather than the numerical keys for the countries.

Solution

Instead of using table import, use free-form query import. In this mode, Sqoop will allow you to specify any query for importing data. Instead of the parameter --table, use the parameter --query with the entire query for obtaining the data you would like to transfer.

Let's look at an example with the normalized table normcities and its dictionary countries. In order to achieve the same output as with importing the denormalized table cities, you could use the following Sqoop command:

```
sqoop import \
  --connect jdbc:mysql://mysql.example.com/sqoop \
  --username sqoop \
  --password sqoop \
  --query 'SELECT normcities.id, \
               countries.country, \
               normcities.city \
               FROM normcities \
               JOIN countries USING(country_id) \
               WHERE $CONDITIONS' \
  --split-by id \
  --target-dir cities
```

Discussion

The free-form query import is one of the advanced features of Sqoop. As with all advanced software features, it gives you great power. With great power comes significant responsibility.

There is a lot to be aware of when using free-form query imports. By using query imports, Sqoop can't use the database catalog to fetch the metadata. This is one of the reasons why using table import might be faster than the equivalent free-form query import. Also, you have to manually specify some additional parameters that would otherwise be populated automatically. In addition to the --query parameter, you need to specify the `--split-by` parameter with the column that should be used for slicing your data into multiple parallel tasks. This parameter usually automatically defaults to the primary key of the main table. The third required parameter is `--target-dir`, which specifies the directory on HDFS where your data should be stored.

The free-form query import can't be used in conjunction with the `\--warehouse-dir` parameter.

Sqoop performs highly efficient data transfers by inheriting Hadoop's parallelism. To help Sqoop split your query into multiple chunks that can be transferred in parallel, you need to include the `$CONDITIONS` placeholder in the where clause of your query. Sqoop will automatically substitute this placeholder with the generated conditions specifying which slice of data should be transferred by each individual task. While you could skip `$CONDITIONS` by forcing Sqoop to run only one job using the `--num-mappers 1` parameter, such a limitation would have a severe performance impact.

Sqoop will concurrently run several instances of your query at the same time for different slices of data. With one straightforward join, this won't be an issue, but it can be an issue for more complex queries.

If your query needs more than a few seconds in order to start sending data, it might not be suitable for the free-form query import. If this is the case, you can always run the expensive query once prior to Sqoop import and save its output in a temporary table. Then you can use table import to transfer the data into Hadoop.

4.2. Using Custom Boundary Queries

Problem

You found free-form query import to be very useful for your use case. Unfortunately, prior to starting any data transfer in MapReduce, Sqoop takes a long time to retrieve the minimum and maximum values of the column specified in the `--split-by` parameter that are needed for breaking the data into multiple independent tasks.

Solution

You can specify any valid query to fetch minimum and maximum values of the `--split-by` column using the `--boundary-query` parameter:

```
sqoop import \
  --connect jdbc:mysql://mysql.example.com/sqoop \
```

```
--username sqoop \
--password sqoop \
--query 'SELECT normcities.id, \
              countries.country, \
              normcities.city \
              FROM normcities \
              JOIN countries USING(country_id) \
              WHERE $CONDITIONS' \
--split-by id \
--target-dir cities \
--boundary-query "select min(id), max(id) from normcities"
```

Discussion

In order to partition data into multiple independent slices that will be transferred in a parallel manner, Sqoop needs to find the minimum and maximum value of the column specified in the `--split-by` parameter. In a table-based import, Sqoop uses the table's primary key by default and generates the query `select min(col), max(col) from tbl` (for table `tbl` and split column `col`). In the case of the free-form query import, there is no table that Sqoop can use for fetching those values; instead, it will use the entire query specified on the command line as a subquery in place of the table name, resulting in a query `select min(col), max(col) from ($YOUR_QUERY)`. Such a query is highly inefficient, as it requires materialization of the output result set prior to moving any data just for the purpose of getting the import boundaries.

Without understanding your query and the underlying data, there aren't many optimizations that Sqoop can automatically apply. Sqoop does offer the parameter `--boundary-query`, with which a custom query can override the generated query. The only requirement for this query is to return exactly one row with exactly two columns. The first column will be considered the lower bound, while the second column will be the upper bound. Both values are inclusive and will be imported. The type of both columns must be the same as the type of the column used in the `--split-by` parameter. Knowing your data and the purpose of your query allows you to easily identify the main table, if there is one, and select the boundaries from this table without any additional join or data transformations.

The query used for fetching boundaries can indeed be arbitrary. Let's walk through a few examples. If you happen to know the boundaries prior to running Sqoop, you can select them directly without opening a single table using a constant boundary query like `SELECT 1, 500`. If you're storing the minimum and maximum values in different tables for accounting purposes, you can fetch the data from there as well. There is no requirement to reference any table used in the `--query` parameter inside the `--boundary-query` parameter. As the output of the boundary query serves as the basis for importing data, it is imperative that the return value not skew the import process.

4.3. Renaming Sqoop Job Instances

Problem

You run several concurrent free-form query imports from various databases at the same time on your Hadoop cluster. All MapReduce jobs are named `QueryResult.jar`, so it's very hard to see which MapReduce job belongs to which imported query.

Solution

You can use the command-line parameter `--mapreduce-job-name` to specify the name of the generated MapReduce job. This name will then show up in the JobTracker web UI. To name your job `normcities`, you would use the following command:

```
sqoop import \
  --connect jdbc:mysql://mysql.example.com/sqoop \
  --username sqoop \
  --password sqoop \
  --query 'SELECT normcities.id, \
                  countries.country, \
                  normcities.city \
                  FROM normcities \
                  JOIN countries USING(country_id) \
                  WHERE $CONDITIONS' \
  --split-by id \
  --target-dir cities \
  --mapreduce-job-name normcities
```

Discussion

Sqoop follows the default behavior of Hadoop in using the submitted JAR name for the MapReduce job name. In a table import, the JAR is named after the table name, resulting in unique JAR and therefore also MapReduce job names. In the free-form query import case, with no single table involved, Sqoop will use `QueryResult` as the base name for the JAR. All query imports will look exactly the same on the JobTracker web UI. You can use the `--mapreduce-job-name` parameter to choose a name for your job.

4.4. Importing Queries with Duplicated Columns

Problem

You have more than one table that you're joining in your free-form query. Your Sqoop import is failing with an error message about duplicate columns, similar to the following one:

```
Imported Failed: Duplicate Column identifier specified: 'id'
```

Solution

You might need to use SQL projection to rename columns in the query so that each column in the output result set has a unique name. You can do that using the AS syntax. For example, to import city names from the tables `cities` and `normcities`, you can use the following query:

```
--query "SELECT \
    cities.city AS first_city \
    normcities.city AS second_city \
  FROM cities \
  LEFT JOIN normcities USING(id)"
```

Discussion

During initial preparation and before submitting the MapReduce job, Sqoop performs several actions. One such action is to fetch metadata about the transferred columns and their associated types. During this step, Sqoop will generate a Java class that contains one attribute for each column that will be named as the column itself. Java attributes must be unique; therefore, all columns in your query must have unique names.

While databases generally enforce unique column names in tables, it is a likely scenario that during a `join` operation two columns from different tables will have the same name. The output result set then contains two columns with the same name. This is especially problematic if your query selects all columns from all join tables using fragments like `select table1.*, table2.*`. In this case, you must break the general statement down, name each column separately, and use the AS clause to rename the duplicate columns so that the query will not have duplicate names.

CHAPTER 5

Export

The previous three chapters had one thing in common: they described various use cases of transferring data from a database server to the Hadoop ecosystem. What if you have the opposite scenario and need to transfer generated, processed, or backed-up data from Hadoop to your database? Sqoop also provides facilities for this use case, and the following recipes in this chapter will help you understand how to take advantage of this feature.

5.1. Transferring Data from Hadoop

Problem

You have a workflow of various Hive and MapReduce jobs that are generating data on a Hadoop cluster. You need to transfer this data to your relational database for easy querying.

Solution

You can use Sqoop's `export` feature that allows you to transfer data from the Hadoop ecosystem to relational databases. For example, to export data from the `export-dir` directory `cities` (the directory in HDFS that contains the source data) into table `cities` (the table to populate in the database), you would use the following Sqoop command:

```
sqoop export \
  --connect jdbc:mysql://mysql.example.com/sqoop \
  --username sqoop \
  --password sqoop \
  --table cities \
  --export-dir cities
```

Discussion

Export works similarly to import, except export transfers data in the other direction. Instead of transferring data from the relational database using SELECT queries, Sqoop will transfer the data to the relational database using INSERT statements. Sqoop's export workflow matches the import case with slight differences. After you execute the Sqoop command, Sqoop will connect to your database to fetch various metadata about your table, including the list of all columns with their appropriate types. Using this metadata, Sqoop will generate and compile the Java class. The generated class will be used in the submitted MapReduce job that will export your data. Similar to the import mode, no data is being transferred through the Sqoop client itself. All transfers are done in the MapReduce job, with Sqoop overseeing the process from your machine.

Sqoop fetches the table's metadata in the export: the destination table (specified with the --table parameter) must exist prior to running Sqoop. The table does not have to be empty, and you can even export new data from Hadoop to your database on an iterative basis. The only requirement is that there not be any constraint violations when performing the INSERT statements (for example, you can twice export the same value for any primary or unique key).

5.2. Inserting Data in Batches

Problem

While Sqoop's export feature fits your needs, it's too slow. It seems that each row is inserted in a separate insert statement. Is there a way to batch multiple insert statements together?

Solution

Tailored for various databases and use cases, Sqoop offers multiple options for inserting more than one row at a time.

First, you can enable JDBC batching using the --batch parameter:

```
sqoop export \
  --connect jdbc:mysql://mysql.example.com/sqoop \
  --username sqoop \
  --password sqoop \
  --table cities \
  --export-dir cities \
  --batch
```

The second option is to use the property sqoop.export.records.per.statement to specify the number of records that will be used in each insert statement:

```
sqoop export \
  -Dsqoop.export.records.per.statement=10 \
  --connect jdbc:mysql://mysql.example.com/sqoop \
  --username sqoop \
  --password sqoop \
  --table cities \
  --export-dir cities
```

Finally, you can set how many rows will be inserted per transaction with the `sqoop.export.statements.per.transaction` property:

```
sqoop export \
  -Dsqoop.export.statements.per.transaction=10 \
  --connect jdbc:mysql://mysql.example.com/sqoop \
  --username sqoop \
  --password sqoop \
  --table cities \
  --export-dir cities
```

The default values can vary from connector to connector. Sqoop defaults to disabled batching and to 100 for both `sqoop.export.records.per.statement` and `sqoop.export.statements.per.transaction` properties.

Discussion

These methods all look at batching from different perspectives that you can combine as you see fit. Let's take a closer look at each of them.

The JDBC interface exposes an API for doing batches in a prepared statement with multiple sets of values. With the `--batch` parameter, Sqoop can take advantage of this. This API is present in all JDBC drivers because it is required by the JDBC interface. The implementation may vary from database to database. Whereas some database drivers use the ability to send multiple rows to remote databases inside one request to achieve better performance, others might simply send each query separately. Some drivers cause even worse performance when running in batch mode due to the extra overhead introduced by serializing the row in internal caches before sending it row by row to the database server.

The second method of batching multiple rows into the same query is by specifying multiple rows inside one single insert statement. When setting the property `sqoop.export.records.per.statement` to a value of two or more, Sqoop will create the following query:

```
INSERT INTO table VALUES (...), (...), (...), ...;
```

As the query is completely generated by Sqoop, the JDBC driver doesn't alter it, sending it to the remote database as is. Unfortunately, not all databases support multiple rows in a single insert statement. Common relational databases like MySQL, Oracle, and PostgreSQL do support this, but some data warehouses might not. There is also one additional drawback that you need to keep in mind when using large numbers of rows inserted with a single insert statement: most databases have limits on the maximum query size. The Sqoop export will fail if the remote database server does not accept the generated query.

The third batching mechanism does not try to achieve better performance by putting multiple rows together as the previous two options did. The value specified in `sqoop.ex port.statements.per.transaction` determines how many insert statements will be issued on the database prior to committing the transaction and starting a new one. Higher values of this property lead to longer-lived transactions and remove the overhead introduced by creating and finishing the transaction. Using higher values usually helps to improve performance. However, the exact behavior depends on the underlying database and its functionality. If your database requires a special table-level write lock for inserting rows into a table, using a higher value for statements per transaction might lead to significantly decreased performance.

As each method uses a different means for improving the export performance, you can combine all of them together. Each database system and user environment is different. There aren't best practices that can be broadly applied across all use cases. Our recommendation is to start with enabling `--batch` import and specify the number of rows per statement to roughly equal the maximum allowed query size. From that starting point, experiment with different values.

5.3. Exporting with All-or-Nothing Semantics

Problem

You need to ensure that Sqoop will either export all data from Hadoop to your database or export no data (i.e., the target table will remain empty).

Solution

You can use a staging table to first load data to a temporary table before making changes to the real table. The staging table name is specified via the `--staging-table` parameter. In the below example, we set it to `staging_cities`:

```
sqoop export \
  --connect jdbc:mysql://mysql.example.com/sqoop \
  --username sqoop \
  --password sqoop \
  --table cities \
  --staging-table staging_cities
```

Discussion

When using a staging table, Sqoop will first export all data into this staging table instead of the main table that is present in the parameter --table. Sqoop opens a new transaction to move data from the staging table to the final destination, if and only if all parallel tasks successfully transfer data. On one hand, this approach guarantees all-or-nothing semantics for the export operation, but it also exposes additional limitations on the database side. As Sqoop will export data into the staging table and then move it to the final table, there is a period of time where all your data is stored twice in the database (one copy in the staging table and one in the final table). You must have sufficient free space on your system to accommodate two copies in order to use this method. As the data is first loaded somewhere else and then moved to the final table, using a staging table will always be slower than exporting directly to the final table.

Sqoop requires that the structure of the staging table be the same as that of the target table. The number of columns and their types must be the same; otherwise, the export operation will fail. Other characteristics are not enforced, as Sqoop gives the user the ability to take advantage of advanced database features. You can store the staging table in a different logical database (on the same physical box) or in a different file group. Some extended attributes do not make a difference to Sqoop: your target table might be partitioned whereas the staging table might not, or both tables might use different storage engines.

Ultimately, it's the user's responsibility to make sure the data export is valid when the tables are not defined in exactly the same way.

The staging table is not automatically created by Sqoop and must exist prior to starting the export process. In addition, it needs to be empty in order to end up with consistent data. You can specify the parameter --clear-staging-table to instruct Sqoop to automatically clean the staging table for you. If supported by the database, Sqoop will use a TRUNCATE operation to clean up the staging table as quickly as possible.

5.4. Updating an Existing Data Set

Problem

You previously exported data from Hadoop, after which you ran additional processing that changed it. Instead of wiping out the existing data from the database, you prefer to just update any changed rows.

Solution

You can take advantage of the update feature that will issue `UPDATE` instead of `INSERT` statements. The update mode is activated by using the parameter `--update-key` that contains the name of a column that can identify a changed row—usually the primary key of a table. For example, the following command allows you to use the column `id` of table `cities`:

```
sqoop export \
  --connect jdbc:mysql://mysql.example.com/sqoop \
  --username sqoop \
  --password sqoop \
  --table cities \
  --update-key id
```

Discussion

The parameter `--update-key` is used to instruct Sqoop to update existing rows rather than insert new ones. This parameter requires a comma-separated list of columns that should be used to uniquely identify a row. All of those columns will be used in the `WHERE` clause of the generated `UPDATE` query. All other table columns will be used in the `SET` part of the query. For example, for a table containing four columns (`c1`, `c2`, `c3`, and `c4`), calling Sqoop with the `--update-key c2,c4` will generate the following update query:

```
UPDATE table SET c1 = ?, c3 = ? WHERE c2 = ? and c3 = ?
```

It's very important to understand the structure of the query to see how the update mode will export data from Hadoop. First of all, the columns used to identify the row will never be updated because they are not part of the `SET` clause. Also, if your data in Hadoop contains some completely new rows, the `WHERE` clause will not match any rows on the database side. Such an operation on the database side is fully valid, but it results in no updated rows. Therefore, new rows are not exported in update mode at all.

5.5. Updating or Inserting at the Same Time

Problem

You have data in your database from a previous export, but now you need to propagate updates from Hadoop. Unfortunately, you can't use the update mode, as you have a considerable number of new rows and you need to export them as well.

Solution

If you need both updates and inserts in the same job, you can activate the so-called upsert mode with the `--update-mode allowinsert` parameter. For example:

```
sqoop export \
  --connect jdbc:mysql://mysql.example.com/sqoop \
  --username sqoop \
  --password sqoop \
  --table cities \
  --update-key id \
  --update-mode allowinsert
```

Discussion

The ability to conditionally insert a new row or update an existing one is an advanced database feature known as upsert. This feature is not available on all database systems nor supported by all Sqoop connectors. Currently it's available only for Oracle and non-direct MySQL exports.

Each database implements the upsert feature a bit differently. With Oracle, Sqoop uses a MERGE statement that specifies an entire condition for distinguishing whether an insert or update operation should be performed. With MySQL, Sqoop uses an ON DUPLICATE KEY UPDATE clause that does not accept any user-specified conditions; it decides whether to update or insert based on the table's unique key.

The upsert feature will never delete any rows: this update method won't work as expected if you're trying to sync data in your database with arbitrarily altered data from Hadoop. If you need to perform a full sync including inserts, updates, and deletes, you should export the entire data set using normal export without any update features enabled. This of course requires an empty output table, so you must truncate it prior to running the export. If you can't do that as your applications are actively using the table, you can temporarily export the data to a different table and then swap the two tables once the Sqoop export is successful.

See Also

MySQL's behavior with upsert mode is further described in Recipe 7.6.

5.6. Using Stored Procedures

Problem

Your database already has a workflow for ingesting new data that heavily uses stored procedures instead of direct INSERT statements.

Solution

You can switch from INSERT statements to stored procedures very easily. Instead of using the --table parameter to specify the target table, use the --call parameter followed by the name of the stored procedure that should be called. In the example below, we use the stored procedure named `populate_cities`:

```
sqoop export \
  --connect jdbc:mysql://mysql.example.com/sqoop \
  --username sqoop \
  --password sqoop \
  --call populate_cities
```

Discussion

Using a stored procedure in Sqoop export is very straightforward. Instead of issuing an INSERT statement, Sqoop will call your stored procedure with the value for each column of the input data as a separate parameter. For example, when exporting into MySQL, Sqoop uses the following query:

```
CALL populate_cities(?, ?, ?)
```

There are a couple of gotchas that you should keep in mind when using stored procedures for export. Sqoop is a specialized bulk transfer tool that will run several concurrent export tasks, all calling stored procedures in a parallel manner. Sqoop does not impose any limitation on the stored procedure complexity. Complex procedures may induce heavy load on the database server, negatively affecting its performance. You are advised to use this feature with a very simple stored procedure or rather prepare the data on the Hadoop side properly so that it can be inserted directly into the final tables, bypassing the advanced logic in the stored procedure.

5.7. Exporting into a Subset of Columns

Problem

You have data in Hadoop that you need to export. Unfortunately, the corresponding table in your database has more columns than the HDFS data.

Solution

You can use the `--columns` parameter to specify which columns (and in what order) are present in the Hadoop data. For example, to limit the export to columns `country` and `city`, use the following command:

```
sqoop export \
  --connect jdbc:mysql://mysql.example.com/sqoop \
  --username sqoop \
  --password sqoop \
  --table cities \
  --columns country,city
```

Note the absence of whitespace with the --columns parameter.

Discussion

By default, Sqoop assumes that your HDFS data contains the same number and ordering of columns as the table you're exporting into. The parameter --columns is used to specify either a reordering of columns or that only a subset of table columns is available in the input files. The parameter accepts a comma-separated list of column names and can be particularly helpful if you're exporting data to different tables or your table has changed between the import and export operations.

There is a limitation to keep in mind when using the --columns parameter while exporting only to a subset of table columns. As Sqoop uses INSERT statements to transfer data from Hadoop, the database must allow inserting new rows with only specified columns.

 Columns that are not being exported must either allow NULL values or contain a default value that your DB engine could use.

5.8. Encoding the NULL Value Differently

Problem

Your Hadoop processing uses custom string constants to encode missing values, and you need Sqoop to properly use them rather than insisting on the default null.

Solution

You can override the NULL substitution characters by setting the --input-null-string and --input-null-non-string parameters to any value. For example, use the following command to override it to \N:

```
sqoop export \
  --connect jdbc:mysql://mysql.example.com/sqoop \
  --username sqoop \
  --password sqoop \
  --table cities \
  --input-null-string '\\N' \
  --input-null-non-string '\\N'
```

Discussion

Similar to import mode, Sqoop in export mode allows you to override the default string constant used for encoding missing values in the database, the so-called NULL value. Sqoop has different parameters for specifying the substitution string for import and export.

The export variants of parameters always start with the word input, whereas the import parameters do not.

Specifically for text-based columns, defined as VARCHAR, CHAR, NCHAR, TEXT, and a few others, you can use the parameter --input-null-string. Independent of this parameter, for all other column data types you can use the --input-null-non-string parameter. Some of the connectors might not support different substitution strings for different column types and so might require you to specify the same value for both parameters.

If, in your workflow, your data is first imported to Hadoop and subsequently exported back, it's important to keep the parameters of the import and associated export job in sync; otherwise, you might end up with failing jobs or even corrupted data. This is especially the case when you're using Sqoop to integrate with a downstream system like Hive that uses different NULL substitution constants.

See Also

Details about NULL substitution characters are described in Recipe 2.10.

5.9. Exporting Corrupted Data

Problem

The input data is not clean. Sqoop fails on the export command with the following exception:

```
java.io.IOException: Can't export data, please check task tracker logs
```

Solution

Check your map task logs to see what is happening. You can view them by opening the JobTracker (or ResourceManager if you're using YARN) web interface and then searching for your Sqoop job.

Discussion

Sqoop export will fail if your data is not in the format that Sqoop expects. If some of your rows have fewer or more columns than expected, you might see that exception. To help you triage the corrupted row, Sqoop will print out very detailed information about the incident into the task log, for example:

```
java.lang.NumberFormatException: For input string: "A"
...
TextExportMapper: On input: A,Czech Republic,Koprivnice
TextExportMapper: On input file: /user/root/corrupted_cities/input.corrupted
TextExportMapper: At position 0
TextExportMapper:
TextExportMapper: Currently processing split:
TextExportMapper: Paths:/user/root/corrupted_cities/input.corrupted:0+1
TextExportMapper:
```

The example shows a corrupted file when we artificially changed the first column of the table cities from an integer constant to the letter A. Sqoop has reported which exception was thrown, in which input file it happened, where exactly in the file it occurred, and finally the entire row that it is currently processing. Unfortunately, Sqoop currently does not offer the ability to skip corrupted rows, so you must fix them prior to running the export job.

CHAPTER 6

Hadoop Ecosystem Integration

The previous chapters described the various use cases where Sqoop enables highly efficient data transfers between Hadoop and relational databases. This chapter will focus on integrating Sqoop with the rest of the Hadoop ecosystem: we will show you how to run Sqoop from within a specialized Hadoop scheduler named Oozie and how to load your data into Hadoop's data warehouse system, Apache Hive, and Hadoop's database, Apache HBase.

6.1. Scheduling Sqoop Jobs with Oozie

Problem

You are using Oozie in your environment to schedule Hadoop jobs and would like to call Sqoop from within your existing workflows.

Solution

Oozie includes special Sqoop actions that you can use to call Sqoop in your workflow. For example:

```
<workflow-app name="sqoop-workflow" xmlns="uri:oozie:workflow:0.1">
    ...
    <action name="sqoop-action">
        <sqoop xmlns="uri:oozie:sqoop-action:0.2">
            <job-tracker>foo:8021</job-tracker>
            <name-node>bar:8020</name-node>
            <command>import --table cities --connect ...</command>
        </sqoop>
        <ok to="next"/>
        <error to="error"/>
    </action>
```

```
    ...
</workflow-app>
```

Discussion

Starting from version 3.2.0, Oozie has built-in support for Sqoop. You can use the special action type in the same way you would execute a MapReduce action. You have two options for specifying Sqoop parameters. The first option is to use one tag, <command>, to list all the parameters, for example:

```
<command>import --table cities --username sqoop --password sqoop ...</command>
```

In this case, Oozie will take the entire content of the <command> tag and split it by spaces into a list of parameters. This list is then passed as is into Sqoop.

It's important to note that Oozie will not do any escaping as in a shell environment. For example, the fragment --table "my table" will be split into three separate parameters: --table, "my, and table". This obviously won't work if any of your parameters themselves contain spaces, so Oozie offers a second way of entering parameters. Instead of using one <command> tag for the entire Sqoop command line, you can use multiple <arg> tags, one for each parameter. The previous example written with <arg> would be:

```
<arg>import</arg>
<arg>--table</arg>
<arg>cities</arg>
<arg>--username</arg>
<arg>sqoop</arg>
<arg>--password</arg>
<arg>sqoop</arg>
...
```

The content of each <arg> tag is considered to be one parameter regardless of how many spaces it contains; this is especially useful for entering queries as <arg>SELECT * FROM cities</arg>, which is considered to be one single parameter. Having spaces inside of a <command> tag might not be obvious, especially when you're using variables to parametrize your workflow. The preferred way to use Sqoop in Oozie is with <arg> tags.

6.2. Specifying Commands in Oozie

Problem

Your Sqoop command line works when directly executed from the command line. You see warnings or exceptions when running from Oozie. Below are several common exceptions:

```
Character parameter '|' has multiple characters; only the first will be used.
Got error creating database manager: java.io.IOException:
                No manager for connect string: "jdbc:teradata..."
```

Solution

You do not need to escape your parameters when using Oozie. All escape sequences and the surrounding single and double quotes must be removed. Consider, for example, the following Sqoop execution in a shell:

```
sqoop import --password "spEci@l\$" --connect 'jdbc:x:/yyy;db=sqoop'
```

Enter it in the following form in order to have the same behavior in Oozie:

```
<command>sqoop import --password spEci@l$ --connect jdbc:x:/yyy;db=sqoop pass:
[<phrase role='keep-together'></command></phrase>]
```

Discussion

This is due to the way Oozie executes Sqoop commands. Normally, when you enter your Sqoop command in a shell like Bash, it will evaluate all the parameters and change them prior to passing them to Sqoop. For example, if you need to use a semicolon (;) in your parameter, you have to escape it in a shell using the backslash (forming \;). Your shell will automatically transform that to a single semicolon prior to passing the parameter to Sqoop. Similarly, you might need to enclose some of your parameters into single or double quotes on the command line to enter parameters with spaces; the shell will remove the enclosing quotes before passing the parameter to Sqoop.

Oozie, on the other hand, does not use a shell to execute Sqoop. It will directly pass all the parameters as they are without any modifications. To get Sqoop to behave the same way, you need to remove all the escaping that you've introduced on account of the shell. One small exception is Oozie's built-in expression language, which will still be interpreted.

6.3. Using Property Parameters in Oozie

Problem

You are using Sqoop parameters entered with -D, for example -Dsqoop.export.state ments.per.transaction=1. However, it seems that they are ignored when you use them in Oozie.

Solution

You need to put property parameters entered with -D in the configuration section of the Sqoop action, for example:

```
<workflow-app name="sqoop-workflow" xmlns="uri:oozie:workflow:0.1">
    ...
    <action name="sqoop-action">
        <sqoop xmlns="uri:oozie:sqoop-action:0.2">
```

```
    <job-tracker>foo:8021</job-tracker>
    <name-node>bar:8020</name-node>
    <configuration>
      <property>
        <name>sqoop.export.statements.per.transaction</name>
        <value>1</value>
      </property>
    </configuration>
    <command>import --table cities --connect ...</command>
  </sqoop>
  <ok to="next"/>
  <error to="error"/>
  </action>
    ...
  </workflow-app>
```

Discussion

Property parameters entered with -D are processed differently than the usual Sqoop parameters. Whereas the normal command-line parameters are passed directly and are fully processed by Sqoop, the property parameters are preprocessed before the Sqoop execution and put into a Hadoop configuration object that Sqoop will load and use. Since Oozie is not using the Sqoop shell script but directly calling the Sqoop binaries, there is no preprocessing stage. The -D parameters are not loaded when they are specified inside the <command> or <arg> tags. Oozie has a very generic way of altering the default configuration object using the <configuration> tag. You need to put all -D parameters that you're using into the configuration section in order to properly propagate them into Sqoop.

6.4. Installing JDBC Drivers in Oozie

Problem

Sqoop works correctly when executed from the command line, but in Oozie it cannot find the JDBC drivers.

Solution

You need to install the JDBC drivers into Oozie separately. You have two options: install the driver either into your workflow's lib/ directory or into the shared action library location usually found at /user/oozie/share/lib/sqoop/.

Discussion

Due to licensing, Sqoop does not ship with any JDBC drivers. You have to manually download the drivers from the applicable vendors' websites and install them into Sqoop, usually by copying the JAR files into the lib/ directory. Oozie doesn't use your local installation of Sqoop, even when it's available on the same machine as the Oozie server. It always uses the version available in its share libs, which is a special location on HDFS where Oozie keeps libraries for special actions. This share lib path is customizable and can be changed in the oozie.service.WorkflowAppService.system.libpath property. The default value is /user/${user.name}/share/lib, where ${user.name} will be substituted with the user that is running the Oozie server.

You have two options for installing the additional JDBC drivers for Oozie. The first and simpler method is to put them directly into the shared lib location in Sqoop's own subfolder (by default, /user/${user.name}/share/lib/sqoop). This directory is shared across all Sqoop actions in all workflows, so you have to do it only once. The second option requires you to install the JDBC driver JAR files separately into each workflow's lib/ directory. As this second method requires multiple copies of the same files, it's preferable to use the shared lib directory instead.

See Also

You can find details about where to retrieve JDBC drivers in Recipe 1.2.

6.5. Importing Data Directly into Hive

Problem

You would like Sqoop to import your data directly into Hive.

Solution

Sqoop supports importing into Hive. Add the parameter --hive-import to your command to enable it:

```
sqoop import \
  --connect jdbc:mysql://mysql.example.com/sqoop \
  --username sqoop \
  --password sqoop \
  --table cities \
  --hive-import
```

Discussion

The biggest advantage of using Sqoop for populating tables in Hive is that it can automatically populate the metadata for you. If the table in Hive does not exist yet, Sqoop will simply create it based on the metadata fetched for your table or query. If the table already exists, Sqoop will import data into the existing table. If you're creating a new Hive table, Sqoop will convert the data types of each column from your source table to a type compatible with Hive. Usually this conversion is straightforward: for example, JDBC types VARCHAR, CHAR, and other string-based types are all mapped to Hive STRING.

Sometimes the default mapping doesn't work correctly for your needs; in those cases, you can use the parameter --map-column-hive to override it. This parameter expects a comma-separated list of key-value pairs separated by the equal sign (=) in order to specify which column should be matched to which type in Hive. For example, if you want to change the Hive type of column id to STRING and column price to DECIMAL, you can specify the following Sqoop parameters:

```
sqoop import \
  ...
  --hive-import \
  --map-column-hive id=STRING,price=DECIMAL
```

During a Hive import, Sqoop will first do a normal HDFS import to a temporary location. After a successful import, Sqoop generates two queries: one for creating a table and another one for loading the data from a temporary location. You can specify any temporary location using either the --target-dir or --warehouse-dir parameter. It's important not to use Hive's warehouse directory (usually /user/hive/warehouse) for the temporary location, as it may cause issues with loading data in the second step.

If your table already exists and contains data, Sqoop will append to the newly imported data. You can change this behavior by using the parameter --hive-overwrite, which will instruct Sqoop to truncate an existing Hive table and load only the newly imported one. This parameter is very helpful when you need to refresh Hive's table data on a periodic basis.

See Also

When you're overriding Hive type, you might also need to override the Java mapping described in Recipe 2.8.

6.6. Using Partitioned Hive Tables

Problem

You want to import data into Hive on a regular basis (for example, daily), and for that purpose your Hive table is partitioned. You would like Sqoop to automatically import data into the partition rather than only to the table.

Solution

Sqoop supports Hive partitioning out of the box. In order to take advantage of this functionality, you need to specify two additional parameters: --hive-partition-key, which contains the name of the partition column, and --hive-partition-value, which specifies the desired value. For example, if your partition column is called day and you want to import your data into the value 2013-05-22, you would use the following command:

```
sqoop import \
  --connect jdbc:mysql://mysql.example.com/sqoop \
  --username sqoop \
  --password sqoop \
  --table cities \
  --hive-import \
  --hive-partition-key day \
  --hive-partition-value "2013-05-22"
```

Discussion

Sqoop mandates that the partition column be of type STRING. The current implementation is limited to a single partition level. Unfortunately, you can't use this feature if your table has more than one level of partitioning (e.g., if you would like a partition by day followed by a partition by hour). This limitation will most likely be removed in future Sqoop releases.

Hive's partition support is implemented with virtual columns that are not part of the data itself. Each partition operation must contain the name and value of the partition. Sqoop can't use your data to determine which partition this should go into. Instead Sqoop relies on the user to specify the parameter --hive-partition-value with an appropriate value.

 Sqoop won't accept a column name for this parameter.

6.7. Replacing Special Delimiters During Hive Import

Problem

You've imported the data directly into Hive using Sqoop's --hive-import feature. When you call SELECT count(*) FROM your_table query to see how many rows are in the imported table, you get a larger number than is stored in the source table on the relational database side.

Solution

This issue is quite often seen when the data contains characters that are used as Hive's delimiters. You can instruct Sqoop to automatically clean your data using `--hive-drop-import-delims`, which will remove all `\n`, `\t`, and `\01` characters from all string-based columns:

```
sqoop import \
  --connect jdbc:mysql://mysql.example.com/sqoop \
  --username sqoop \
  --password sqoop \
  --table cities \
  --hive-import \
  --hive-drop-import-delims
```

If removing the special characters is not an option in your use case, you can take advantage of the parameter `--hive-delims-replacement`, which will accept a replacement string. Instead of removing separators completely, they will be replaced with a specified string. The following example will replace all `\n`, `\t`, and `\01` characters with the string SPECIAL:

```
sqoop import \
  --connect jdbc:mysql://mysql.example.com/sqoop \
  --username sqoop \
  --password sqoop \
  --table cities \
  --hive-import \
  --hive-delims-replacement "SPECIAL"
```

Discussion

Sqoop will, by default, import data into comma-separated text files where each line represents one row. However, if your data contains the new-line character (`\n`), such a row will create two separate lines that will consequently be processed as two separate rows by Hive. Consequently, Hive will show a higher row count than your source table. Other default parameters like `\t` and `\01` might also cause parsing issues; however, the new-line character is the most common issue. You can instruct Sqoop to clean up your data either with `--hive-drop-import-delims` or `--hive-delims-replacement` parameters.

Even though both parameters contain `hive` in their names, they are not restricted to working in tandem with the `--hive-import` parameter. They can be used in any import job using text files to ensure that the output files have one line per imported row. Also, as they target the default delimiters, using them with custom delimiters is not recommended, as they will always remove or substitute only the default delimiters.

6.8. Using the Correct NULL String in Hive

Problem

You've imported your data into Hive using Sqoop and now you're trying to query it. However, you can see that some columns contain the correct NULL value but some contain the string literal null and are not selected using the expression column IS NULL.

Solution

Due to differences in the default NULL substitution string between Sqoop and Hive, you have to override the Sqoop default substitution strings to be compatible with Hive. For example:

```
sqoop import \
  --connect jdbc:mysql://mysql.example.com/sqoop \
  --username sqoop \
  --password sqoop \
  --table cities \
  --hive-import \
  --null-string '\\N' \
  --null-non-string '\\N'
```

Discussion

Hive, by default, expects that the NULL value will be encoded using the string constant \N. Sqoop, by default, encodes it using the string constant null. To rectify the mismatch, you'll need to override Sqoop's default behavior with Hive's.

This issue with different NULL substitution strings is very tricky to debug. Depending on the way Hive parses data, it seems to be working sometimes and at other times does not. When Hive is not able to parse certain columns, it will return NULL instead of throwing an exception and failing the entire query execution. Let's investigate this a bit further with an example. Consider the following table:

```
CREATE TABLE tbl(id int, txt varchar(50));
INSERT INTO tbl VALUES (NULL, NULL);
```

The table tbl has two columns, one numeric and one text, with a row that has NULL stored in both columns. Without any special parameters, Sqoop will import this table as a file with a single row null,null.

When Hive reads this line, it will first separate each column using the comma as a separator. Subsequently, it will start processing the value for each column. The first column is of type int and contains the string constant null, which is not a valid number value. Instead of throwing a parsing exception at this point, Hive will substitute NULL for this cell. The second column is of type string and contains the string constant `null`, which is a fully valid string value. It's returned as is without any conversion to `NULL`. The result can be seen in the following example:

```
hive> SELECT * FROM tbl;
NULL  null
```

Similarly, when you export data from Hive into your relational database, you should use the parameters `--input-null-string` and `--input-null-non-string` and set both to value \N. Table 6-1 contains a list of recommended parameters for `NULL` substitution strings for both import and export:

Table 6-1. Recommended parameters for import and export

Import	Export
`--null-string '\\N'`	`--input-null-string '\\N'`
`--null-non-string '\\N'`	`--input-null-non-string '\\N'`

See Also

Details about `NULL` substitution strings are described in Recipes 2.10 and 5.8.

6.9. Importing Data into HBase

Problem

Instead of importing data into an HDFS file or a Hive table, you would like to transfer it into HBase, Hadoop's real-time database.

Solution

Sqoop has out-of-the-box support for HBase. To enable import into HBase, you need to supply two additional parameters: `--hbase-table` and `--column-family`. The parameter `--hbase-table` specifies the name of the table in HBase to which you want to import your data. The parameter `--column-family` specifies into which column family Sqoop will import your table's data. For example, you can import the table `cities` into HBase with the same table name and use the column family name `world`:

```
sqoop import \
  --connect jdbc:mysql://mysql.example.com/sqoop \
  --username sqoop \
  --password sqoop \
  --table cities \
  --hbase-table cities \
  --column-family world
```

Discussion

To insert data into HBase there are three mandatory parameters: the table name, a column family name within the table, and the id of the row into which you are inserting data. Sqoop uses one table and one column family per import job, so you have to specify them using the --hbase-table and --column-family parameters on the command line. Unlike importing into Hive, Sqoop does not use a default table name when importing into HBase. Rather, you have to specify a valid table name with the --hbase-table parameter.

To identify each individual row in HBase, Sqoop defaults to the column name specified in the --split-by parameter or the column that was automatically identified to serve this purpose (usually the primary key of the table). You can override this behavior using the --hbase-row-key parameter.

Each input row from your source table will be transformed into a single PUT operation and inserted into HBase. Each column except the row key will be converted into text and inserted as a cell value.

 Both the HBase table and the column family must exist prior to running the Sqoop import command. If you want Sqoop to create the table automatically, you'll need to specify the parameter --create-hbase-table.

6.10. Importing All Rows into HBase

Problem

You've imported your table directly into HBase, but it seems that there are fewer rows than in your source table.

Solution

You might need to enable inserting the row key into the value using the property sqoop.hbase.add.row.key, for example:

```
sqoop import \
  -Dsqoop.hbase.add.row.key=true \
  --connect jdbc:mysql://mysql.example.com/sqoop \
  --username sqoop \
  --password sqoop \
  --table cities \
  --hbase-table cities \
  --column-family world
```

Discussion

HBase does not allow the insertion of empty values: each cell needs to have at least one byte. Sqoop serialization, however, skips all columns that contain a NULL value, resulting in skipping rows containing NULL value in all columns. This explains why Sqoop imports fewer rows than are available in your source table. The property `sqoop.hbase.add.row.key` instructs Sqoop to insert the row key column twice, once as a row identifier and then again in the data itself. Even if all other columns contain NULL, at least the column used for the row key won't be null, which will allow the insertion of the row into HBase.

6.11. Improving Performance When Importing into HBase

Problem

Imports into HBase take significantly more time than importing as text files in HDFS.

Solution

Create your HBase table prior to running Sqoop import, and instruct HBase to create more regions with the parameter NUMREGIONS. For example, you can create the HBase table `cities` with the column family `world` and 20 regions using the following command:

```
hbase> create 'cities', 'world', {NUMREGIONS => 20, SPLITALGO => 'HexString
Split'}
```

Discussion

By default, every new HBase table has only one region, which can be served by only one Region Server. This means that every new table will be served by only one physical node. Sqoop does parallel import of your data into HBase, but the parallel tasks will bottleneck when inserting data into one single region. Eventually the region will split up as it fills, allowing Sqoop to write to two servers, which does not help significantly. Over time, enough region splitting will occur to help spread the load across your entire HBase cluster. It will, however, be too late. Your Sqoop import by then has already taken a significant performance hit. Our recommendation is, prior to running the Sqoop import, create the HBase table with a sufficient number of regions to spread the load across your entire HBase cluster.

CHAPTER 7

Specialized Connectors

Due to its versatility, Sqoop transfers data from a variety of relational database systems, such as Oracle, MySQL, PostgreSQL, and Microsoft SQL Server, as well as from enterprise data warehouses, such as Netezza and Teradata. While working with these database systems, you may encounter issues specific to a system vendor. This chapter guides you through common installation, connection, and syntax issues.

7.1. Overriding Imported boolean Values in PostgreSQL Direct Import

Problem

PostgreSQL direct imports boolean values as TRUE or FALSE strings. If your subsequent processing expects different values, you need to override those defaults.

Solution

Specify the extra parameters --boolean-true-string and --boolean-false-string to override the default value to a different string. For example, to use 0 for false and 1 for true, you could use the following Sqoop command:

```
sqoop import \
  --connect jdbc:postgresql://postgresql.example.com/database \
  --username sqoop \
  --password sqoop \
  --direct \
  --table table_with_booleans \
  -- \
  --boolean-true-string 1 \
  --boolean-false-string 0
```

Discussion

The PostgreSQL direct connector uses the `COPY (SELECT QUERY) TO STDOUT` clause for retrieving data from your database that will by default use the string constants `TRUE` and `FALSE` when importing data from `Boolean` and `Bit` columns. The PostgreSQL direct connector only supports import and delegates the export to the nondirect JDBC connector. Therefore, both parameters, `--boolean-true-string` and `--boolean-false-string`, are applicable only to import and will be ignored during export operation.

See Also

The reason for the extra `--` between the Sqoop arguments and extra arguments is explained in Recipe 1.4.

7.2. Importing a Table Stored in Custom Schema in PostgreSQL

Problem

You are taking advantage of custom schemas in PostgreSQL and you need Sqoop to import and export tables from there.

Solution

Use the extra parameter `--schema` for specifying a custom schema name. For example, to import data from table `cities` stored in schema `us` you can use the following command:

```
sqoop import \
  --connect jdbc:postgresql://postgresql.example.com/database \
  --username sqoop \
  --password sqoop \
  --table cities \
  -- \
  --schema us
```

Discussion

Sqoop does not have a notion of custom schemas, and so it supports only tables stored in the default schema named `public`. You need to specify the parameter `--schema` with a schema name if your table is stored in a different schema. Alternatively, you can include your custom schema in the `search_path` for the user account that you're using for Sqoop. For example, to set the default search path to schemas `public` and `us` for user `sqoop`, you would execute the following query to the PostgreSQL server:

```
ALTER USER sqoop SET search_path = public,us;
```

7.3. Exporting into PostgreSQL Using pg_bulkload

Problem

You are using the `pg_bulkload` utility to load data to your PostgreSQL server. Since Sqoop utilizes `mysqlimport` for MySQL, can Sqoop also utilize `pg_bulkload` for PostgreSQL?

Solution

Sqoop offers a specialized connector for PostgreSQL that takes advantage of the `pg_bulkload` utility. You can use the following Sqoop command to make use of this connector:

```
sqoop import \
  --connect jdbc:postgresql://postgresql.example.com/database \
  --username sqoop \
  --password sqoop \
  --connection-manager org.apache.sqoop.manager.PGBulkloadManager \
  --table cities
```

Discussion

`pg_bulkload` is a third-party utility not distributed with PostgreSQL. You need to manually download and install it. It allows a user to load data into a PostgreSQL server at a high speed by bypassing the write-ahead log and shared buffers. Using the `pg_bulkload` utility with Sqoop is very simple, as Sqoop has built-in support for it.

As with other direct connectors, you need to have the `pg_bulkload` utility available on all nodes in your Hadoop cluster because Sqoop's tasks can be executed on any Task-Tracker node. You can specify the path to the utility with the `pgbulkload.bin` property. For example, if you installed the utility in `/usr/local/bin/pg_bulkload`, you can use the following Sqoop command:

```
sqoop import \
  -Dpgbulkload.bin=/usr/local/bin/pg_bulkload \
  --connect jdbc:postgresql://postgresql.example.com/database \
  --username sqoop \
  --password sqoop \
  --connection-manager org.apache.sqoop.manager.PGBulkloadManager \
  --table cities
```

See Also

More information about `mysqlimport` for MySQL is in Recipe 2.7.

7.4. Connecting to MySQL

Problem

While importing data from MySQL, Sqoop throws an exception about a communication failure:

```
ERROR manager.SqlManager: Error executing statement:
com.mysql.jdbc.exceptions.jdbc4.CommunicationsException:  Communications  link
failure
```

Solution

First, rule out connectivity and permission issues for the user to access the database over the network. You may need to set the property `interactiveClient=true` in the JDBC connection string or increase the value for the `wait_timeout` property on the MySQL server side.

Discussion

Verify that you can connect to the database from the node where you are running Sqoop by using the following command in your shell:

```
mysql --host=<IP Address> --database=test --user=<username>
--password=<password>
```

If this works, it rules out any problem with the client network configuration or security/ authentication configuration. Please note that Sqoop will also require database connectivity from all nodes in your Hadoop cluster.

The MySQL configuration option `wait_timeout` can cause connections to close when they are idle for too long. As Sqoop is reusing the same connection on the client side, you might experience communication failures if the value of `wait_timeout` property is too low. One solution is to set the property `interactiveClient=true` in the JDBC connection string, which uses an alternative timeout period. Another solution is to increase the value for the `wait_timeout` property on the MySQL side.

7.5. Using Direct MySQL Import into Hive

Problem

You are using direct import from MySQL into Hive. You've noticed that the Hive shell correctly displays NULL values as the string NULL; however, you are not able to select those rows using the IS NULL condition in queries.

Solution

You need to disable direct import and use the JDBC method by omitting the `--direct` parameter, so that you can instruct Sqoop to use Hive-specific NULL substitution strings. For example:

```
sqoop import \
  --connect jdbc:mysql://mysql.example.com/sqoop \
  --username sqoop \
  --password sqoop \
  --table cities \
  --hive-import \
  --null-string '\\N' \
  --null-non-string '\\N'
```

Discussion

The MySQL direct connector uses a native utility called `mysqldump` to perform a highly efficient data transfer between the MySQL server and Hadoop cluster. This utility unfortunately does not support using custom NULL substitution strings and will always import missing values as a string constant NULL. This is very confusing on the Hive side, as the Hive shell will display the value as NULL as well. It won't be perceived as a missing value, but as a valid string constant. You need to turn off direct mode (by omitting the `--direct` option) in order to override the default NULL substitution string.

See Also

More details about NULL values are available in Recipes 2.10 and 5.8.

7.6. Using the upsert Feature When Exporting into MySQL

Problem

You've modified data sets in Hadoop and you want to propagate those changes back to your MySQL database. Your transformations both update existing rows and create new ones. While using Sqoop's upsert functionality in the `--update-mode allowinsert` parameter, you notice that Sqoop doesn't use any of the columns specified in `--update-key` in order to determine whether to update an existing row or insert a new one.

Solution

You need to create a unique key on all columns that you are going to use with the `--update-key` parameter. For example, to create a unique key on the column `city` of the `cities` table, you would execute the following MySQL query:

```
ALTER TABLE cities ADD UNIQUE KEY (city);
```

Discussion

The MySQL database does not support the MERGE SQL operator as Oracle does. Instead, MySQL provides the ON DUPLICATE KEY UPDATE clause that Sqoop uses when exporting in upsert mode. The MERGE operator allows you to specify a condition to determine whether an update or insert operation should be performed. MySQL's clause will always try to insert. Only if the insert fails because such an operation would violate a unique key constraint does it update the existing row instead. Since MySQL does not allow you to specify a condition, the table's unique key is always used. Since Sqoop uses the ON DUPLICATE KEY UPDATE clause, columns specified in the --update-key parameter are not used for determining what operation should be performed. This is quite confusing, as you always have to specify this parameter in order to enable update mode, yet the columns are not used in upsert mode.

See Also

The functionality of upsert and its Sqoop implementation are further explained in Recipe 5.5.

7.7. Importing from Oracle

Problem

Sqoop can't find any columns when importing data from Oracle. For example, you see the following exception:

```
java.lang.IllegalArgumentException: Attempted to generate class with no columns!
```

Solution

Make sure that both the table and the username are specified with the correct case. Usually, specifying both the table and usernames in uppercase will resolve this issue. In addition, if a different user created the transferred table, you will need to specify this user in the --table parameter in the form user.table_name. For example, to import table cities created by user kathleen from Oracle using user sqoop, you would execute the following Sqoop command:

```
sqoop import \
  --connect jdbc:oracle:thin:@oracle.example.com:1521/ORACLE \
  --username SQOOP \
  --password sqoop \
  --table KATHLEEN.cities
```

Discussion

The Oracle connector uses the following catalog query for retrieving table structure information (number of columns, their names, and associated data types):

```
SELECT COLUMN_NAME FROM ALL_TAB_COLUMNS
WHERE OWNER = ? AND TABLE_NAME = ? ORDER BY COLUMN_ID
```

As the equals operator is case sensitive, you must enter both the table name and owner in the same way as is recorded in the database catalog.

 By default, Oracle will automatically uppercase all table and user-names if they are not explicitly enclosed in double quotes during creation. Sqoop will use the current username if you don't specify the explicit table owner inside the --table parameter.

7.8. Using Synonyms in Oracle

Problem

You need to import or export an Oracle table using a synonym rather than a real table name.

Solution

In order to reference Oracle synonyms, you need to switch to the Generic JDBC Connector because the specialized Oracle connector does not support them. You can instruct Sqoop to use the Generic JDBC Connector by specifying the parameter --connection-manager with the full class name of the connector. For example, to import synonym CIT, you would use the following Sqoop command:

```
sqoop import \
  --connect jdbc:oracle:thin:@oracle.example.com:1521/ORACLE \
  --username SQOOP \
  --password sqoop \
  --table CIT \
  --driver oracle.jdbc.OracleDriver \
  --connection-manager org.apache.sqoop.manager.GenericJdbcManager
```

Discussion

The built-in Oracle connector queries the catalog object ALL_TAB_COLUMNS in order to retrieve a table's column names and associated data types. Unfortunately, Oracle is storing synonyms in a different catalog object and thus the Connector can't fetch the metadata properly, resulting in import or export failure.

The Generic JDBC Connector does not use catalog tables and views, and so it doesn't have issues with synonyms. Instead it will issue a query with the clause `WHERE 1=0` that won't transfer any data as the condition is always false but will return correct metadata for transported data. Returned metadata will contain the basic information required, like column count, names, and associated types; however, it lacks any advanced information like whether the table is partitioned or not. Although the Generic JDBC Connector works quite nicely here, it can't take full advantage of your database server.

7.9. Faster Transfers with Oracle

Problem

Sqoop does a great job transferring data between Oracle and Hadoop. Is there a faster and more optimal way of exchanging data with Oracle?

Solution

You should consider using OraOop, a specialized connector for Oracle developed and maintained by Quest Software, now a division of Dell. You can download the connector from the Cloudera website (*http://bit.ly/19FMsxo*).

Discussion

OraOop is a highly specialized connector for the Oracle database. Instead of splitting data into equal ranges using one column (usually the table's primary key), OraOop utilizes the concept of `rowid`. In doing so, the connector ensures that no two parallel running tasks will read data from the same Oracle block. This lowers disk operations on the database server, significantly improving performance. You are encouraged to download, install, and use the OraOop connector instead of the built-in one.

See Also

Detailed instructions about the installation of special connectors are covered in Recipe 1.3.

7.10. Importing into Avro with OraOop

Problem

You are importing a table containing a `DATE` column from Oracle database into Avro format, but you're getting the following exception:

```
org.apache.avro.UnresolvedUnionException: Not in union ["long","null"]:
```

Solution

You have two options to overcome this issue. The first is to set the property oraoop.timestamp.string to the value false to disable OraOop's default date-to-string mapping.

```
sqoop import \
  -Doraoop.timestamp.string=false \
  --connect jdbc:oracle:thin:@oracle.example.com:1521/ORACLE \
  --username SQOOP \
  --password sqoop \
  --table cities \
  --as-avrodatafile
```

The second option is to map all DATE columns to String using the --map-column-java parameter. For example, if your table contains two DATE columns, namely CREATED and UPDATED, you would use the following Sqoop command:

```
sqoop import \
  -Doraoop.timestamp.string=false \
  --connect jdbc:oracle:thin:@oracle.example.com:1521/ORACLE \
  --username SQOOP \
  --password sqoop \
  --table cities \
  --as-avrodatafile \
  --map-column-java CREATED=String,UPDATED=String
```

Discussion

Avro encoding doesn't have an indicator to say which field is next. It just encodes one field after another and in the order they appear in the schema definition. Since there is no way for the parser to know that a field has been skipped, there is no such thing as an optional field in Avro. Instead, if you want to be able to leave out a value, you can use a union type, like union { null, long }. Unions are encoded with an extra byte to inform the parser which of the possible union types to use, followed by the value itself. By making a union with the null type, you can make a field optional. Sqoop uses unions to encode database NULL values. In every generated Avro schema, all columns are encoded as a union of null with a real type in order to allow correct processing of missing values.

When importing into an Avro file, Sqoop represents DATE values as type Long, so Avro schema union { null, long } will be generated. However, OraOop automatically converts all DATE values into String, and String can't be stored inside the union { null, long } Avro schema, resulting in the Not in union exception. There are two options to work around this behavior. The first is to disable the implicit mapping to String in OraOop by setting the property oraoop.timestamp.string to the value false. The second option is to force Sqoop to generate a different schema by mapping all DATE columns into String as OraOop expects.

7.11. Choosing the Proper Connector for Oracle

Problem

You are not sure when to use OraOop, the built-in Oracle connector, or the Generic JDBC Connector.

Solution

For the best performance, use the OraOop connector. If OraOop does not work for your use case, the next best alternative is the built-in connector. If those two connectors do not work in your environment, your last resort is the Generic JDBC Connector.

 The Generic JDBC Connector is slower than even the built-in Oracle Connector.

Discussion

There are three connectors available for use when you need to transfer data to or from the Oracle database: the Generic JDBC Connector, the built-in Oracle connector, and OraOop. The Generic JDBC Connector and the built-in Oracle connector are bundled within Sqoop, and you can use them out of the box. OraOop is not distributed with Sqoop, and you would need to manually download and install it.

The JDBC driver is a dependency for all three connectors. You will always need to install the JDBC driver. Sqoop will automatically try to use the most optimal connector available, so OraOop will be used automatically when it's installed. If you need to conditionally disable OraOop on a per-job basis, you can set the property oraoop.dis abled to true. For example, use the following command to disable OraOop after it's been installed:

```
sqoop import \
  -Doraoop.disabled=true \
  --connect jdbc:oracle:thin:@oracle.example.com:1521/ORACLE \
  --username SQOOP \
  --password sqoop \
  --table cities
```

If you would prefer to explicitly choose which connector will be used rather than the implicit selection, you can do that using the following set of parameters.

Choose the OraOop connector:

```
sqoop import \
  --connection-manager com.quest.oraoop.OraOopConnManager \
  --connect jdbc:oracle:thin:@oracle.example.com:1521/ORACLE \
  --username SQOOP \
  --password sqoop \
  --table cities
```

Choose the built-in Oracle connector:

```
sqoop import \
  --connection-manager org.apache.sqoop.manager.OracleManager \
  --connect jdbc:oracle:thin:@oracle.example.com:1521/ORACLE \
  --username SQOOP \
  --password sqoop \
  --table cities
```

And finally, choose the Generic JDBC Connector:

```
sqoop import \
  --connection-manager org.apache.sqoop.manager.GenericJdbcManager \
  --driver oracle.jdbc.OracleDriver \
  --connect jdbc:oracle:thin:@oracle.example.com:1521/ORACLE \
  --username SQOOP \
  --password sqoop \
  --table cities
```

7.12. Exporting into Teradata

Problem

You are doing a Sqoop export to Teradata using the Generic JDBC Connector and it fails with the following exception:

```
Syntax error: expected something between ')' and ','.)
```

Solution

Set the parameter -Dsqoop.export.records.per.statement=1:

```
sqoop export \
  -Dsqoop.export.records.per.statement=1 \
  --connect jdbc:teradata://teradata.example.com/DATABASE=database \
  --username sqoop \
  --password sqoop \
  --table cities\
  --export-dir cities
```

Discussion

Sqoop, by default, creates INSERT statements for multiple rows in one query, which is a quite common SQL extension implemented by most of the database systems. Unfortunately, Teradata does not support this extension, and therefore you need to disable this behavior in order to export data into Teradata.

See Also

Property `sqoop.export.records.per.statement` was further described in Recipe 5.2.

7.13. Using the Cloudera Teradata Connector

Problem

You have a Teradata appliance as your enterprise data warehouse system and you need to import and export data from there to Hadoop and vice versa. You have used Sqoop with the Generic JDBC Connector. Is there a more optimal solution?

Solution

Download, install, and use the Cloudera Teradata Connector, which is available for free on the Cloudera website (*http://www.cloudera.com/downloads*).

Discussion

The Cloudera Teradata Connector is a specialized connector for Teradata that is not part of the Sqoop distribution. You need to download and install it manually. This connector takes advantage of Teradata FastLoad and FastExport over JDBC to provide the best available performance when transferring data. You should install this connector if you need to transfer data with Teradata.

See Also

Detailed instructions about the installation of special connectors are covered in Recipe 1.3.

7.14. Using Long Column Names in Teradata

Problem

Table-based import is failing with an exception about an invalid name:

```
[Error 3737] [SQLState 42000] Name requires more than 30 bytes in LATIN
internal form.
```

Solution

You can use SQL projection to rename all columns longer than 28 characters to have a maximum of 28 characters. For example, to rename the column REALLY_LONG_COL UMN_NAME_30CHAR to a shorter name, you can use the --query import instead of the --table import.

```
sqoop import \
  --connect jdbc:teradata://teradata.example.com/DATABASE=database \
  --username sqoop \
  --password sqoop \
  --query "SELECT REALLY_LONG_COLUMN_NAME_30CHAR AS shorter_column_name \
            FROM table"
```

Discussion

Teradata has an internal 30-character limit on the column and table names. Some of the Teradata technologies and tools prepend each column name with a special prefix that counts toward the 30-character limit. In the case of using FastLoad over JDBC, the effective limit is 28 characters as the Teradata JDBC driver automatically adds a prefix V_ to each column. As this limitation is imposed by Teradata itself, there is not much that Sqoop can do besides allow you to use the Generic JDBC Connector instead of the Cloudera Teradata Connector.

Using the Generic JDBC Connector will significantly decrease performance.

About the Authors

Kathleen Ting is a customer operations engineering manager at Cloudera, where she helps customers deploy and use the Hadoop ecosystem in production. She has spoken on Hadoop, ZooKeeper, and Sqoop at many big data conferences, including Hadoop World, ApacheCon, and OSCON. She's contributed to several projects in the open source community and is a committer and PMC member on Sqoop.

Jarek Jarcec Cecho is a software engineer at Cloudera, where he develops software to help customers better access and integrate with the Hadoop ecosystem. He has led the Sqoop community in the architecture of the next generation of Sqoop, known as Sqoop 2. He's contributed to several projects in the open source community and is a committer and PMC member on Sqoop, Flume, and MRUnit.

Colophon

The animal on the cover of *Apache Sqoop Cookbook* is the Great White Pelican (*Pelecanus onocrotalus*).

The cover image is from *Meyers Kleines*. The cover font is Adobe ITC Garamond. The text font is Adobe Minion Pro; the heading font is Adobe Myriad Condensed; and the code font is Dalton Maag's Ubuntu Mono.

Get even more for your money.

Join the O'Reilly Community, and register the O'Reilly books you own. It's free, and you'll get:

- $4.99 ebook upgrade offer
- 40% upgrade offer on O'Reilly print books
- Membership discounts on books and events
- Free lifetime updates to ebooks and videos
- Multiple ebook formats, DRM FREE
- Participation in the O'Reilly community
- Newsletters
- Account management
- 100% Satisfaction Guarantee

Signing up is easy:

1. **Go to: oreilly.com/go/register**
2. **Create an O'Reilly login.**
3. **Provide your address.**
4. **Register your books.**

Note: English-language books only

To order books online:

oreilly.com/store

For questions about products or an order:

orders@oreilly.com

To sign up to get topic-specific email announcements and/or news about upcoming books, conferences, special offers, and new technologies:

elists@oreilly.com

For technical questions about book content:

booktech@oreilly.com

To submit new book proposals to our editors:

proposals@oreilly.com

O'Reilly books are available in multiple DRM-free ebook formats. For more information:

oreilly.com/ebooks

O'REILLY®

Spreading the knowledge of innovators   oreilly.com

CPSIA information can be obtained at www.ICGtesting.com
Printed in the USA
BVOW01s0000230114

342773BV00003B/13/P

9 781449 364625